games 3

THE ideas LIBRARY

FOR YOUTH GROUPS

THE IDEAS LIBRARY

games 3

THE ideas LIBRARY

FOR YOUTH GROUPS

Youth Specialties

ZONDERVAN™

A DIVISION OF HARPERCOLLINS*PUBLISHERS*

Games 3 for Youth Groups

Copyright © 2001 by Youth Specialties

Youth Specialties Books, 300 S. Pierce St., El Cajon, CA 92020, are published by Zondervan Publishing House, 5300 Patterson Ave. S.E., Grand Rapids, MI 49530.

Library of Congress Cataloging-In-Publication Data

Games 3 for youth groups / Youth Specialties
    p. cm. – (Ideas Library)
  Includes index.
  ISBN 0-310-23179-5
  1. Group games. 2. Outdoor games. 3. Youth—Recreation. I. Title: Games three for youth groups. II. Youth Specialties (Organization) III. Series

  GV1203 .G2142 2001
  790.1'922—dc21

                         00-50330

Unless otherwise indicated, all Scripture quotations are taken from the *Holy Bible: New International Version* (North American Edition). Copyright © 1973, 1978, 1984 by International Bible Society. Used by permission of Zondervan Publishing House.

Ideas in this book have been voluntarily submitted by individuals and groups who claim to have used them in one form or another with their youth groups. Before you use an idea, evaluate it for its suitability to your own groups, for any potential risks, for safety precautions that must be taken, and for advance preparation that may be required. Youth Specialties and Zondervan Publishing House are not responsible for, nor have any control over, the use or misuse of this book.

Edited by Casey Finley, Laura Gross, and Lorna McFarland Hartman
Writing contributions by Laura Gross
Cover design by Curt Sell
Interior layout by Tom Gulotta
Illustrations by Paz Design
Printed in the United States of America

02 03 04 05 06 07 / VG /10 9 8 7 6 5 4 3

CONTENTS

So what killer game have you invented lately?

Are your kids still talking about that game you invented for last month's party? Youth Specialties pays $40 (and in some cases, more) for unpublished, field-tested ideas that have worked for you.

You've probably been in youth work long enough to realize that sanitary, theoretical, tidy ideas aren't what in-the-trenches youth workers are looking for. They want—*you* want—imagination and take-'em-by-surprise novelty in parties and other events. Ideas that have been tested and tempered and improved in the very real, very adolescent world you work in.

So here's what to do:
- Sit down at your computer, get your killer game out of your head and onto your hard drive, then e-mail it to Ideas@YouthSpecialties.com. Or print it off and fax it to 619-440-4939 (Attn: Ideas).
- If you need to include diagrams, photos, art, or samples that help explain your game, stick it all in an envelope and mail it to our street address: Ideas, 300 S. Pierce St, El Cajon, CA 92020.
- Be sure to include your name and all your addresses and numbers.
- Let us have about three months to give your game idea a thumbs up or down.*

*Hey, no offense intended if your idea isn't accepted. It's just that our fussy Ideas Library editor has these *really* meticulous standards. If the game isn't creative, original, and just plain fun in an utterly wild or delightful way, she'll reject it (reluctantly, though, because she has a tender heart). Sorry. We figure you deserve only the best game ideas.

FOR LARGE GROUPS

These games are geared toward groups of thirty or more and are designed to be played in a gymnasium, fellowship hall, or similar room. But no matter how large your group is or what the confines of your meeting area are, you'll find crowd breakers, mixers, and contests that will work for you.

AMPUTEE BALLOON SWAT

You remember the rainy-day game that boredom drove you to—Keep the Balloon from Hitting the Ground or Else It Blows Up. For this version, each person has an inflated balloon to protect—and at the same time, they must try to bat others' balloons to the ground. The catch is, they can use only one hand to play this game. They have to keep the other hand in a pocket or behind their back or otherwise out of play. You get the idea—one hand to share both defensive and offensive tasks.

You'll need boundaries of some sort—such as walls or tape strips on the floor—to keep all players in the thick of the action so they don't wander off to protect their balloons. Players are out when their balloons hit the floor or are swatted out of bounds. Or you can add the rule that players are out only when their balloons hit the floor and are stepped on and popped—and they can only step on a balloon that's already on the ground. *Paul J. Cronenwett*

BALLOON SOCCER

While your next youth event is winding down, use up those leftover balloons with a quick game of Balloon Soccer. Any size, color, or number of inflated balloons will work. Designate a goal area at each end of the room, which no one may enter during the game. Place all the balloons in the center of the room, and split the group into two teams. One group stands on each side of the balloons.

Each team tries to move the balloons into the other team's goal area using only their feet. Once a balloon has been corralled inside an end zone, it can't be put back into play. Players who step into the end zone must take one minute out of play. The game ends when all the balloons are behind the goal lines. The winner is the team with the fewest balloons inside their own goal. If you wish, the winning team may be allowed to celebrate their victory by popping all the balloons any way they want to. *Len Cuthbert*

CHAIR BALLOON BALL

A smooth, non-carpeted floor works best for this fast-moving game—it helps eliminate the shocking element of static electricity! Create two even teams of students and have each group choose a goalie. Give each person a balloon to inflate and leave in a big box along the sidelines. Then ask each player to grab a chair before the game begins. Players should arrange their chairs in the playing area like positions on a real soccer field, with the two goalies sitting at opposite ends.

Two opposing players face off with one balloon to begin the game. The teams play regular offense and defense, but there are a couple of twists to the rules. Team members can move anywhere on the playing field, but their chairs must remain underneath them at all times. So they use one hand to hit the balloon and the other to hold onto their chair.

The second twist involves the goalies. When a balloon is passed to a goalie, that person's job is to sit on it and try to pop it before the other team loudly counts to three. If the goalie fails to pop the balloon, the balloon should be returned to the center of the field and put back into play.

A point is scored whenever a goalie pops a balloon, and then a new balloon is tossed onto the center of the field for the next round of the game. Once all the balloons are mere fragments of their former selves, the team with the most balloon bits under the goalie's chair is declared to be the winning team! *Troy Smith*

CANDY-COATED TEAMS

Tired of having your students number off for every team competition—"One, two, three, one, two, three…"? Place a piece of Skittles candy in a dark-colored balloon and inflate it—one balloon per student. As your students arrive, give each person a balloon. Instruct kids to pop the balloons however they like, as long as they save the surprise inside. In other words, no eating the surprise until you say it's okay!

After they've retrieved their pieces of candy, players should mingle and find their teammates (students with the same color candy). There are five original flavors of Skittles, so if you need more than five teams for a game, you could also use M&Ms, Reese's Pieces, or another kind of hard-shell candy.

Larry Marshall

MARSHMALLOW MIDGET BALL

Locked out of the sports equipment closet again? Don't even *have* a sports equipment closet? Then try raiding the church kitchen and playing a few

innings of this short—but not necessarily quick—game. Two teams play a good old-fashioned game of baseball, using jumbo-size marshmallows for the ball (you'll want to have a large bag of these on hand) and a spatula for the bat. Use whatever stationary objects you have handy for the bases—wastepaper baskets, chairs, orange safety cones, or adult leaders.

Just before the first pitch is thrown, casually mention that players must play the game on their knees. At this point you may want to move the bases a little closer together or provide kneepads for the batting team. Points are scored whenever a runner—crawler—safely reaches home base.

A final twist to the all-American game—if a fielder catches a fly marshmallow in her mouth and eats it (with no help from hands), then it counts as *two* outs. *Yvette Lansdowne*

MARSHMALLOW TOSS ACROSS

Before playing this quirky game of catch, players number off and arrange themselves as shown in the diagram below, each person standing on a chair. Once the students are in position, they should pair

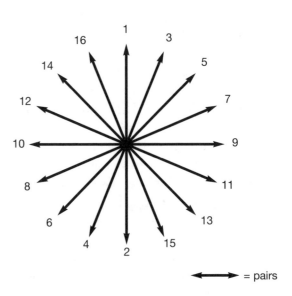

◄———► = pairs

off with the people standing directly across the circle from them. Every twosome will compete against the other twosomes to win.

Even-numbered players each get a Styrofoam cup full of mini marshmallows (each cup should contain the same amount). The odd-numbered play-

14

ers each get an empty cup to use to try to catch the marshmallows.

When you give the signal, the marshmallow tossers hurl marshmallows—one at a time—to their partners. No matter how wild the toss, players aren't allowed to step off their chairs during the game or points will be deducted from their final score. When a team runs out of marshmallows, both players should sit down. The first team to sit gets five bonus points, the last team loses five points.

After everyone is seated, the catchers count the marshmallows in their cups and give their teams one point per marshmallow. The pair with the fewest marshmallows at the end of a round earns the dreaded pick-up penalty—they must pick up all the mashed marshmallows off the floor. Play again with tossers and catchers trading places. *Len Cuthbert*

MYSTERY CLUE HUNT

With this game, you can simultaneously add a little mystery to your youth meeting and foster a sense of teamwork among your students. Players work together in smaller groups, searching for clues and trying to solve a five-part mystery.

Copy down the following 25 sample clues—or come up with your own—and write each one on a slip of colored paper. Clues from the same category should be written on the same color of paper.

Category: The Criminal (pink paper)
• The first
• Chop chop: no lies
• The Delaware
• Not Bill Clinton
• He could have used Polident

Category: The Crime (purple paper)
• The 10 Commandments
• First to second is easiest, rarely at home
• A furry scarf
• Number 8
• Rabbits and foxes and minks—oh my!

Category: The Item (tan paper)
• Another name for a sports stadium
• It can be an island thing, with chili
• Fevered canine

• Mustard, no relish
• Who knows what's in it?

Category: The Victim (blue paper)
• It's not easy being this way
• His creator is dead
• His girlfriend is a real porker
• It's time to get things started
• You might find his legs in a fancy restaurant

Category: The Location (yellow paper)
• Fairy tales
• A castle and a mouse
• Lots of cameras
• When you wish upon a star
• Wait forever, then go very fast

The answer is *George Washington stole* a *hot dog* (or Coney) *from Kermit the Frog* at *Disney World* (or Disneyland).

Hide the clues throughout the building—or in areas that have yet to be declared off limits by your church elders—and be creative. Tape them to the backs of pews, onto the blades of ceiling fans, under the toilet tank in the restroom, inside the silverware drawer in the kitchen—no place is too weird!

Read the first paragraph of **The Crime Scene** (page 16) aloud to the group and then give each team of six to eight students a copy of the sheet and a pen or pencil to use during their search. Instruct the groups to look around the building for clues and to leave clues where they find them.

If a group gets stuck during the game, give them a little hint. Tell them that clues found on the same color paper belong in one of the five clue categories and should be used together to solve one of the parts of the mystery. So, using our example, you could tell them that clues about the criminal's identity are all written on pink paper.

When a team thinks they've solved the mystery, they should report back to you or another staff member. If their answer is wrong, they must wait at least three minutes before guessing again. Teams are allowed only three guesses each. Even after a team finally gives the correct answer, let the others continue to work until they've run out of guesses or solved the crime.

Award a mysterious edible prize to the first team

The Crime Scene

A crime has been committed, and it's *your* job to find out **who** did it, **what** they did, **how** they did it, **to whom** they did it, and **where** it all took place. Clues are scattered throughout the building.

The first team to return with *all* the correct answers gets a prize. You must wait at least three minutes between incorrect guesses—and you get only three tries, so your team should be absolutely certain before making your guess.

The Criminal: _____

The Crime: _____

The Item: _____

The Victim: _____

The Location: _____

Your team's answer: _____!

that solves the mystery, like Whatchamacallit candy bars or a box of chocolate-covered candies *without* the list that identifies the contents of each piece.
Brian Morgan

SARDINES FOR CASH

Spice up that old hide-and-seek game of Sardines for your group—all it takes is a wad of play money. Give one player, the banker, a pack of fake cash and one minute to hide. Everyone else waits at the bank (designated location where they can't see the banker's efforts to hide) until you give the signal for the hunt to begin.

Every player who finds the banker gets one dollar and hides with the banker. When you signal that time is up, all players—whether or not they've found the banker—should race back to the bank. The last person to get there loses a dollar. If no one finds the banker during a round, then he gets to keep a dollar for himself.

Play a few rounds. The player with the most play money at the end of the game can cash it in for an edible prize. Or for a twist, let everyone with money cash it in for an edible prize—letting players choose their prize in order of how much money they have. *Len Cuthbert*

DUNGEON KEEPER

There's nothing like a good game of hide-and-seek to help kids let off a little steam. And there's probably nothing your students would enjoy more than a chance to tear around the church in the dark. So give them a chance to do so—in a controlled way, of course.

Begin by telling the players which rooms are strictly off limits during the game, then select someone to be the dungeon keeper. Shut her in a room by herself and have her count to 30 while the other players run and hide, turning off the lights as they go.

After the dungeon keeper is finished counting, she should search room by room—leaving the lights off as she does so. When she finds someone, that person must remain in the room until she has finished searching it for other players. Once the dungeon keeper is convinced she has found everyone in

a particular room, she may turn on the light. If she happened to miss someone who was hiding there, that person should come out when the lights come on. Then all the people who were hiding in that room—whether or not they were caught—are free to run and hide again, turning off the lights as they go. The dungeon keeper should once again count to 30 before resuming her search.

However, if the dungeon keeper successfully catches every player hiding in a room, when the light is turned on they're all out of the game and she's free to move on to search the next dark location. As she progresses through the building, she can mark her progress by leaving doors open and lights on as she exits each room. The last person caught becomes the new dungeon keeper for the next round. *Deborah King*

GOTCHA!

Pit guys against girls for this game in the dark. On each side of the room place a chair with an item underneath it. The same thing should be under both chairs—a hymnbook, a pencil, a candy bar, a CD jewel case, a freshman girl, whatever.

Form a girls' team and a guys' team, one on each side of the room, then turn off the lights. Playing guys versus girls makes for easier team identification and refereeing in the dark. On your signal, players try to retrieve the object from under the opposing team's chair and place it on the seat of *their* team's chair back on the other side of the room. The catch is, teams must play on their hands and knees. (This helps prevent serious injuries in the dark.)

Another twist is that players aren't allowed to touch their opponents. So when the unavoidable happens and opposing team members happen to touch, both players try to be the first to yell, "Gotcha!" to eliminate the opponent from the game. Undoubtedly, there will be frequent disputes over who said "Gotcha!" first, so have staff members on hand to make a judgment call when needed.

Whenever players hear, "Gotcha!" all the players must return to their own sides of the room and start groping in the dark all over again. Even if a player is holding the object and is almost back to his side of the room, he's still required to put the item back under the other team's chair and return to his side of the room.

The first team to nab the other team's object and return to their chair without hearing "Gotcha!" wins. *Troy Smith*

MONTANA HOOPS

When your youth group budget for new equipment has run out, here's a game you can play with just a couple of trashcans and some slightly flat playground balls. The object of the game is to make more goals than your opponents do, and goals are made by throwing the balls into your team's trashcan.

Divide your group into either two or four even teams. Have the members of each team stand in a line across one side of the playing field. Teams should stand directly across the playing field from one another, facing outward so they're facing their own goals (see diagram). Each team should choose a goalie to catch balls in the trashcan. She needs to stay within the designated end zone area, but she's allowed to move the goal in order to catch the balls thrown by her team. Goalies cannot touch balls

B team's goalie   B endzone

cones are good for setting up boundaries

D team's goalie

D endzone

playing field

C endzone

C team's goalie

A team's goalie   A endzone

T) trash cans

balls

Note: for 2 teams, don't set up endzones C & D

with their hands at any time. If a ball lands within a goalie's zone, she puts it back into play by kicking it onto the playing field.

Give each team a ball and signal the start of the game. Players can move anywhere they want to (except end zones), block shots, grab balls away from

their opponents, pass balls to their teammates, and shoot balls into their goals for points. The only thing they cannot do is *move* while they're holding a ball. Instead, they must freeze where they are and try to pass the ball to a teammate. Players who move with the ball or enter any end zone must finish that round on their knees.

When a ball lands in a trashcan, it stays there until all the other balls are also out of play. Points are given to any team that has one or more balls in their trashcan—five points per ball. Whoever has the most points wins the round.

After the scores have been tallied, the teams return to their starting places along the perimeter of the playing field. The balls are retrieved, and each team gets one for the next round. The team who wins the most rounds wins the game. *Alan and Cindy Akana*

STAR WARS

All you need for this chaotic game are some boxes of aluminum foil and a strobe light. Before you play, get your volunteer staff and students to help you make as many aluminum foil balls as they can. Divide the room into quadrants, separate the kids into four even teams—one per section of the room—and give each team a supply of metallic ammunition. You set the time limit for each game.

The object of the game is to remove all the foil balls from your quadrant while staying on your feet—no kneeling! Turn off the lights, turn on the strobe light, and let the chaos begin! The team with the fewest number of balls in its square when the lights come on is the winner. *PB*

STAR WARS DODGE BALL

Here's a dodge ball variation for die-hard science-fiction fans among your students or adult staffers. You'll need lots of balls or other soft objects (like rolled-up socks), a play sword, and the *Star Wars* movie soundtrack.

One player on each team is chosen to be the Jedi warrior and is given a sword—a cardboard tube from wrapping paper, a wiffle bat, a yardstick, or anything that won't hurt when it hits people. Divide the playing area, the ammunition, and your group of students in half. Each team must stay on their side during the game.

Give the signal, and let the balls start flying! For an added special effect, play the *Star Wars* theme song. If a player gets hit by The Dark Side—the other team—she's frozen. Only her Jedi warrior can unfreeze her with a touch of the sword. The object of the game is to freeze your opponent's Jedi warrior quickly so he can't unfreeze his teammates after they're hit. The team with the most players still moving at the end of a round wins.

PRIEST

Here's a variation on the old Battle-Ball game. Two equal teams stand on opposite sides of the room. Each team dresses one member in an old choir robe or some other priestly-looking garment, making that player the priest.

The object of the game is to throw balls—five or six per team—at the other team and try to hit them. However, if a player throws a ball and the other team catches it, the thrower is busted! And the same is true if a player is hit by a ball thrown by the opposing team. When players are out, they must drop to the ground wherever they're standing and play dead. Before tagged players can return to the game, the priests must lay hands on them.

Here's where the theology of the game breaks down: If the priests are hit, they're out of the game for good. After the kids figure out how valuable the priests are, they'll do everything they can to protect them, but they aren't allowed to touch them. Players who are tagged after their priest is out of the game are also permanently eliminated. Once everyone on a team is out, you have a winner. *Broc Jahnke*

LAZARUS BALL

To begin the game, have two to four teams of players line up against the walls—one team per wall. Along the center dividing line, place some playground balls, Nerf soccer balls, or foam footballs—one for every four or five players.

After you give the signal, everyone should race toward the balls—and the battle begins. If a player is hit by a ball, that person is out. If an opponent catches or deflects a ball with the ball in her own hands, the ball-thrower is out. Ousted players should immediately sit down wherever they were when eliminated. They can stand up and return to the game when a teammate touches them with a ball.

This game can go on forever, and there are no winners or losers. Because it's so exhausting for the students, it's a great lock-in activity. *Paul Canady*

TP TANGO

Players stand in a circle with one person in the center. Hand a roll of toilet paper to a student in the circle, and tell him to try to hit the player in the middle with it. When the toilet paper hits the floor, other players can pick it up and throw it again.

Once the center player is hit by the TP, that person should exchange places with the person who threw the TP. Add one or two rolls during play to heighten the challenge. *Len Cuthbert*

MURDER BALL

Two teams face each other in a divided room. Use rolls of toilet paper for the balls in this dodge ball-type game. When a player is hit below the waist with TP that person is out. The team with one or more players left in the game wins. Make the losing team clean up. *Len Cuthbert*

19

TP WAR

Buy a mega-pack of cheap toilet paper. Set up chairs, tables, and other obstacles throughout the room, and draw some boundary lines around the playing area that teams can't cross. Divide the kids into two teams, and evenly distribute the rolls of toilet paper.

Now let the kids start throwing! If a player is hit in the arm, she can no longer use that arm during that round. If she's hit in the leg, she can't use that leg and should drag it behind her, and so on. You'll have to put your kids on the honor system, unless you can think of a way to make the toilet paper leave a mark when it hits! Head shots are not encouraged and therefore don't count as hits.

For potentially fatal injuries—hits on both arms or both legs, or a hit in the stomach or chest—players should report to a referee (adult leader), who makes up a silly penalty for them to perform before they may reenter the game. This could be anything, like making a kid pretend he's a ballerina for one minute or making him do five cartwheels around the room.

You may want to try variations such as:
- Teams play on their knees.
- Each team sets up a target that the other team must hit in order to win.
- One person from each team is chosen to be the general. Wrap each general from shoulders to ankles with masking tape sticky side out. If a general gets a roll of toilet paper stuck to her during the game, her team automatically loses. Or give generals clean plungers to balance on their heads. If a plunger gets knocked off, that team is flushed.

No one really wins this game. It's just a blast to throw a roll of toilet paper at someone. *Chad W. Wintringham*

HUNCHBACK FLUSH

Choose someone to be your Quasimodo, strap a wastebasket to that person's back (keeping the top of the basket at shoulder level), and give him some protective eye gear to wear. Then give the rest of your group rolls and rolls of toilet paper to shoot toward the basket. You can even soak the rolls in water ahead of time to add to the fun and challenge of the game!

The TP throwers should stay 10 to 20 feet away from the hunchbacked player while they're trying to hit the basket. However, Quasi is allowed to move from side to side, forward or backward, and duck his head if necessary—anything to try to catch his teammates' rolls of TP in the basket.

You can set up a competition between however many teams you choose. Just designate a time limit for the TP tossing, and whichever team gets the most rolls into their basket before the time runs out wins. Or forget the competition and just sit back and enjoy the show as the hunchbacked players dodge and weave to try to catch the flying toilet paper rolls! *Ken Lane*

FOUR SQUARE CONE WAR

Divide the room into four sections. Place an orange safety cone in each corner of the room and mark off a two-foot area around each cone. Split the students into four teams, one per section.

The object of the game is to hit the other teams' cones with a ball while protecting your own. Teams must stay in their own quadrants and at least two feet away from their cones at all times. The cones don't have to be

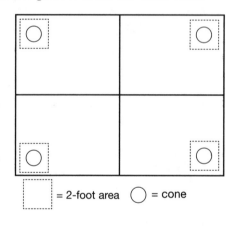

knocked over, only touched by balls. Teams that are out may still participate by trying to help other teams win.

Equally distribute soft playground balls among teams, and let them go. When a ball hits a cone, the cone should be tipped onto its side as a reminder that the team in that quadrant is out. The last team with a cone still standing wins the round.

After each round the teams should rotate and play the next round in different quadrants. An easy way to end the game is to stop play when the teams have played in all four quadrants. The team that wins the most rounds is the champion. *Jim Augustine*

Glowing Goal Toss

Play this game in the dark in a playing area marked with glow-in-the-dark tape. Use two shoeboxes as goals, placing them at opposite ends of the playing area. Mark off a five-foot area around each goal that's off-limits for every player. Divide the group into two teams, and hand out two colors of glow-in-the-dark wristbands for players to wear—one color for each team.

As play begins, each team should try to get some glowing object—a ball, a Frisbee, or a plastic ring—into their opponent's shoebox. Players cannot run while the glowing object is in their possession. It must be passed from player to player and from one end of the room to the other. When the object is on the floor or in the air, it's anyone's ball (or Frisbee or plastic ring), but it can't be stolen from another player. The team that scores the most goals is the winner. *Len Cuthbert*

Shoebox Shuffle Soccer

This game is an indoor version of soccer, but players wear a shoebox on each foot. Unless you have a large stash of old shoeboxes in your supply closet, ask your students to bring two shoeboxes with them to youth group. You'll also need 10 to 12 small Nerf balls and a roll of masking tape to mark the field of play and to tape ripped shoeboxes. Make a center dividing line on the floor and create a goal at each end of the room. Decide how many goals will win the game.

During the game, players must slide or shuffle their feet in order to move around the field. If a player accidentally steps out of a box, she must stop and get it back on her foot before resuming play. If a player's box rips, he can go to the penalty box along the sidelines and get it taped up by an adult leader. No player, including the goalie, can use hands during the game.

Each ball that's kicked into the opponent's goal scores a point for the kicker's team. The first team to score the limit wins the game. *Cindy Allen*

Booty Beach Ball

Stretch a volleyball net, rope, or some other type of divider across the middle of the room, and hang blankets over it so players can't see the other side. Have two teams take their places on either side of the net. All the players should spread out and sit down on their rear ends so they cover the entire area on their side of the divider. Players may not hold or catch the ball, and when the ball hits the ground, the other team scores a point.

To begin the game, put a large inflated beach ball into play by tossing it to the players on one side of the divider. Players can use any part of their bodies to hit the ball as often as necessary to get it back over the divider. The ball can also be hit off the ceiling, stage, walls, stereo—even adult leaders. The round of play stops only when the ball hits the ground. Players can hit the ball as many times as needed to get it over the net, but the same person can't hit it twice in a row.

Points are scored with every serve or volley. Set a score limit of 15 or 21 points for each match. After three matches, the team with the best two-out-of-three record is the ultimate booty-kicking champion! *Joel Lusz*

Wall Ball

For this exciting game, you need a beach ball and a large playing area with four empty walls (meaning it's okay to bounce a ball off them). Divide your group into two teams and assign each a wall for scoring. If you're playing with a smaller group in a full-size gym, the half-court line can serve as an imaginary fourth wall (so if the ball is hit over the center line, the team scores a point). If you have a very large group, use more than one ball to keep the action moving.

To start the game, throw the ball into the air from the middle of the playing field. Players try to knock the ball into their wall to get points. Team members can move anywhere inside the four walls, but they can only hit the ball with their heads or hands—no kicking. They may catch the ball or pick it up from the floor, but they can't run with it. When a point is scored, the ball is taken back to the middle and thrown into the air. *Jerry Weber*

Bouncy Ball Blitz

Divide into four teams and position one group in each corner of the room—preferably a room with a noncarpeted floor. Situate your staff around the perimeter of the room and give each of them 50 to 100 Superballs—those rubber balls that bounce really high. Assign each type of ball a different point value. For example, red ones are worth 10 points, green ones are worth 15, orange ones are worth 500, and so on. Choose a captain for each team whose job it will be to stand outside the play area, receive balls from teammates, and tally the team's score.

On your signal, the leaders simultaneously throw all of the balls into the middle of the room so they bounce all over the place. As soon as the balls are airborne, the kids try to collect as many as they can, bringing them back to their team captain to score points for their team.

After all of the balls have been captured and the scores totaled, return the balls to the adults and start again. Use a new set of point values for the balls in each round. *Aaron Dicer*

Totally Berserk Missile Target Practice

Fill several piñatas with candy, confetti, T-shirts, flyers for upcoming events, CDs, and other goodies. Just be careful about what you put into the piñatas because what goes up must come down! Hang them at least 20 feet above the floor.

Depending on how many piñatas you have, divide your students into teams of 10 or so. Tell them that if a person breaks open a piñata, that person's team can have whatever is inside. But instead

Ninja Yo-Yo

What could you make with only six rubber bands and a Nerf ball? How about a Ninja yo-yo—a springy device for tagging your opponents during any of a number of rousing games!

To create this nifty piece of game equipment, double-wrap one rubber band around the Nerf ball. Then weave the other five rubber bands in a chain (or as many as you like) attached to the band that is wrapped around the ball (see diagram).

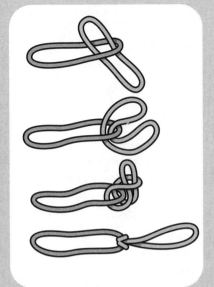

To use it, a player loops the last rubber band in the chain around her finger and then swings the Nerf ball to try to tag her opponents.

Or if you prefer free-for-all games, arm all your students with Ninja yo-yos and show them how to shoot the Nerf ball by looping the last rubber band around your index finger, pulling back on the Nerf ball with your other hand, and letting it fly! The kids can divide into two teams and shoot these harmless Nerf missiles at each other until time is called. Whichever team ends up with the least number of Nerf balls on its side of the room is the champion. *Corby Blem*

of using baseball bats, provide a box of tennis balls, other soft balls (but not softballs) or finger blasters for the kids to use. Crank up some wild music and have your camcorder ready. *Rob Baird*

Mercenaries

Arm several teams of five or fewer players with some type of weapon—an old sock with half a cup of flour behind a knot in the toe, Koosh balls, paper wads, peashooters, whatever. Each player also needs a set of playing chips—checkers, poker chips, beads, or buttons.

During the game teams roam the room in packs. When one team meets up with another team, the two teams face off to try to eliminate each other. To do this, each player on a team pairs off with someone from the other team and tries to tag that person with ammunition first. When a player is hit, that person is out *just* for that face-off and must surrender a chip to the winner. A player who has tagged an opponent finds a new partner to face off with, and the round ends when one team has tagged out all members of the other team. After a face-off ends, the two groups separate and look for other teams to challenge.

Explain the rules of fair play, depending on the type of weapon you choose to use. Teams must meet a set number of opponents before challenging teams they've faced before (teams can't keep playing the easiest opponent over and over).

Players can keep playing as long as they hold chips in their hands. When a player has lost all her chips, she cannot participate in any more face-offs until her team wins new play chips and distributes some to her.

If the number of players on a team becomes greater than the total number of chips the team is holding, the team should have someone sit out during a face-off. For example, if there are four team members but only two chips in a team's possession, then only two team members may participate in that particular face-off. Have adult staff members wander around to keep an eye out for students who are trying to play without enough chips.

Limit the time or the number of chips a player can accumulate to force teams to drop out and end the game. At the end, the team with the most chips wins. *Keith Turner*

POOL-NOODLE FENCING

Cut a foam pool noodle in half to make two harmless fencing swords. Each player needs a sword to play. Students pair off and stand facing each other with their foam weapons in one hand, keeping their other hands behind their backs during the match.

To score points against an opponent, a player must tag his partner in the zone—anywhere between the shoulders and the waist. The first five hits made in an opponent's zone win the round. Eliminated players should leave the floor, while the remaining players pair off and fence again.

Keep doing this until only two players are left to fight. Whoever wins this final bout shall be declared the Pool Noodle Fencing champion! *Jonathan Dixon*

I'M AN EGG

In this version of the question, the egg came first. To play, everyone gets down on his or her haunches and waddles around yelling, "I'm an egg! I'm an egg!" When one player bumps into another, the two eggs play rock-paper-scissors. The winner of the match becomes a chicken and the loser has to waddle off to find another egg to play with.

Chickens continue to waddle around, but now they flap their arms and say, "I'm a chicken, I'm a chicken." When two chickens find each other, they also play rock-paper-scissors. The winner of this contest becomes a dinosaur (by standing up and opening and closing her hands above her head to look like dinosaur jaws), and the loser goes back a step in this food chain and becomes an egg—"egg-ain."

The winner of a prehistoric rock-paper-scissors match between dinosaurs becomes an X-man, complete with Wolverine's razor-sharp claws to indicate the new status. The winning X-man becomes a heckler who is allowed to stop playing the game and sit back to watch peers waddle, chomp, and claw their way through the rest of the game.

The key is that as players win rock-paper-scissors matches, they go up the food chain—so to speak—and face off with others of their kind until they can retire as hecklers. However, every time someone loses a match—at any level—that person must go back to being a lowly egg.

ROCK-PAPER-SCISSORS DRAGON

Pair off your students for some rock-paper-scissors match-ups. The best two out of three wins the match, and the winner becomes the head of the dragon. Meanwhile the loser grabs onto the winner's shoulders or waist and follows wherever the winner goes.

The new dragon heads should challenge each other with three more rounds of rock-paper-scissors. The dragon who loses the match now latches on behind the winner.

This process of elimination continues until there are only two dragons remaining. The final match is an extended three-out-of-five round to determine the fire-breathing champion. *Rev. Sandy Moy Liu*

CLOTHESPIN COLOR WAR

Buy some spring-action clothespins so you have two or more per player. A day or two before you play this game, spray paint half of the clothespins one color and the other half a different color, say red and blue.

Divide your youth group into a boys' team and a girls' team, or divide the group in half if you don't have equal numbers of each gender. Give each member of one team a blue clothespin and each member of the other team a red clothespin. Set a time limit for the game.

Players try to get rid of their clothespins by clipping them onto their opponents while avoiding being clipped by the other team. Make some ground rules regarding the various no-pinning zones—for example, the face and other obvious off-limits areas on the body.

When you call time, the kids should stop right where they are, unclip all the clothespins that are clipped to them, and put the clothespins on the ground in a little pile for counting. The team with the fewest number of clothespins from the *other* team clipped to them wins the game. *Mary Fletcher*

WHO'S GOT MY SHOES?

This game for middle school students requires no prep work or props. Tell the players to take off their shoes, throw them into a big pile in the middle of the room, and then back about 10 feet away from the shoe pile.

At your signal, players run to the pile and grab two unmatched shoes that don't belong to them. After carefully placing both shoes on their feet, the kids should sit down and wait.

Once everyone is wearing two shoes, tell the teenagers they must find and retrieve their own shoes as quickly—and nicely—as they can. The first person to reclaim both shoes and get them back onto their feet is the winner. *Teresa Foster*

AROUND THE WORLD

To begin, the entire youth group should stand in a circle and hold hands. Break one set of linked arms, put a plastic hula hoop over them, and reconnect the hands. The object of the game is to get the hoop passed around the circle. Students can go through it or do whatever else they want, but they must never let go of each other's hands.

Give a reasonable time limit for each round based on the size of your group. For the first try you should overestimate the amount of time you think it will take the hoop to make it around. After that you can have a bonus round with a much shorter time limit and let the group try to beat the clock.

Once your kids get the hang of it, make smaller circles of students and have them compete against one another to see which team can get their hula hoop "around the world" first. *Troy Smith*

KNIGHTS, CAVALIERS, HORSEMEN

Pair everyone off and ask the kids to create two concentric circles with one member of each pair in the inner circle and the other member in the outer circle. Have the inside circle face the outside circle. Blow a whistle or start playing some music to signal the start of the game. Now the inner circle begins walking in a clockwise motion and the outer circle moves counterclockwise.

When you call out "Knights!" players should quickly team up with their new partner and one student sits on the other's knee. If you call out "Cavaliers!" players must jump into the arms of their partners. And if you call out "Horsemen!" one person from each pair gets down on his hands and knees so the other partner can sit on his back. Have pairs hold each position for about 20 seconds and then ask the students to return to their circles and start walking again.

The last pair to follow any command during a round is out of the game and should leave the circles. Randomly repeat commands until only one pair is left. *Troy Smith*

POOL-NOODLE SWAT

This game is similar to Duck Duck Goose, but "It" works from inside the circle. Cut a foam pool noodle into two pieces and use one half as a swatter.

Players take their seats in a large circle of chairs with one chair sitting in the middle. The person chosen to be "It" starts the game by walking around the inside of the circle and swatting a seated player on the arm. Now the game kicks into high gear as "It" runs to the middle of the circle, drops the swatter on the chair, and races back to sit in the vacant chair that once belonged to the newly swatted player. "It" must try to do all of this before the swatted player can get up, grab the swatter from the chair, and swat "It" in return. If "It" succeeds, the swattee goes to the middle. If not, "It" they must try again by swatting a new player.

As your group gets better at playing this game, make the circle bigger and add more swatters, which means there will be more people in the middle and more confusion for everyone! *Jonathan Dixon*

Popcorn String

This game can be adapted for any size group. Pop lots of popcorn ahead of time. Break the kids into teams and line each team up side by side. Hand the first and last person in each line a sewing needle (cross-stitch needles with the bigger holes work well) and a length of dental floss as long as the line of kids. Have the kids hold the line and designate the middle of the floss with a clothespin.

At the count of three, have both ends of each team start stringing the popcorn as fast as they can. The idea is for the team to move the popcorn up the line toward the middle and fill up the string as fast as possible. Let the kids know they can use creative techniques to get the corn to the middle. There are two ways you can designate a winner: by calling time and seeing which team has more popcorn on the string or by seeing which team fills up its line first. This is a great teamwork activity or icebreaker for your group!

Poor Man's Crab Soccer

This game can be played with up to 50 people using one ball. Mark a large court with goals on the walls and ceiling using easily visible tape. Appoint a staff scorekeeper. Divide your group into two, three, or four teams. Players must play in a crab position (on their hands and feet with their faces toward the ceiling). They kick the ball around the court—they can only move the ball around with their feet—and try to hit the goals on the walls and

ceiling. As an added incentive, give more points for goals that are harder to hit. For more action, use two or more balls. *Heath Kumnick*

Dragon Ball

You'll need a large area to run around in and three to five dodgeballs to play this game. For every 15 players, make a six-person dragon. Ideally, start with at least two dragons. Players within the dragon—excluding the first person, who is the dragon's head—must keep both hands on the shoulders of the person in front of them. The players who are not dragons are peasants.

Peasants throw balls at the dragon. The dragon's head throws balls back at the peasants. If a peasant is hit, he or she is considered eaten and must join the dragon at the tail. If the dragon is hit, the player who was hit must drop out of the dragon and become a peasant. Dragons can also attack each other. Once a dragon is down to three people, it's considered killed.

To win the game, choose one or more of the following options.
• Players kill all the dragons.
• The last dragon left alive wins.
• The last peasant left alive wins.
• The first dragon to be 20 people long wins.
You can also make up your own challenges. *Brian Stegner*

Dragon Battle

Dragon Battle is a hilarious variation on Dragon Ball. Since you'll divide your players into three groups, you'll need three colors of balloons and a ball of twine. Each player gets two balloons of the same color.

Each group forms a conga line, with players' hands on the shoulders of the person in front of them. Tie balloons along the players' sides at waist level, one on each player's left and one on the right. The color of the balloons identifies which dragon it is—one color per dragon.

Now choose four people—two near the front of the dragon and two near the back—to be the dragon's claws. These four players only have to hold on with one hand, while with their other hand they claw at other dragons' balloons to pop them and defend their own dragon's balloons. Be sure to stagger the claw hands so there's one clawing on the left side of the dragon and one clawing on the right. When all of a dragon's balloons are popped, it's dead. The last dragon left alive wins.

Brian Stegner

SWARM

At least 45 players are needed for this game. You'll need about 300 small balloons for this size of group—100 each of three different colors. Divide your players into three teams. Each team must appoint a Queen, a Healer, and three Guards. The rest of the team will be Warriors. Use a different balloon color for each team.

Blow up all the balloons, and tie one to each Warrior's ankle. Tie five balloons to the Queen's ankle and three to each Guard's ankle. The Healer has no balloons. The balloon can be as tight or as loose as the player desires, but it must be on the ankle, not up on the leg—and must touch the ground if forced down.

Assign three nest areas equidistant from each other. The space between nests should be as long as possible. The Queen stays in the nest, protected by the Guards. The Healer also stays in the nest with balloons and string. The Healer can't be killed, and the Queen can't move or protect herself. She must stay in one place without moving. The object of the game is to kill the other teams' Queens. This is done by popping all the Queen's balloons—the task of the Warriors. Since Guards have three balloons, it's hard for Warriors to get past them without losing their one balloon right away.

Warriors can pop anyone's balloons as long as their balloon is intact. Once it's popped, they must return to the nest and visit the Healer, who will tie a new balloon on the fallen warrior. Warriors can't replace their own balloons. The Healer also can't heal Guards or protect or heal the Queen.

If a team's Queen is killed, the Healer must join the victorious team and help their Healer. The last team whose Queen is alive wins the game. *Brian Stegner*

CANDY BAR WAR

This is a riot for youth leaders! Most of the leaders will be tempters. You'll need flour, nylons, small candy bars (a dozen or so per adult), and masking tape. Cut off the legs of the nylons. Put a bunch of flour in the foot of each nylon leg, and tie it off. It makes a great little club. You want one club per tempter. Next, tempters tape candy bars all over their clothes and then hide with their clubs. You'll need someone to explain the game to the kids and someone else to run the prison.

Have a leader explain the game to the kids this way: Tempters are roaming around with candy bars taped to their clothes. If the kids want the candy bars, they have to go after them. It's a riot to stop explaining right there and just warn them vaguely about "the consequences." Then bring the kids to the field of play and set 'em loose!

If players are hit, they're thrown into prison (use a church van or back room). They get out of prison by memorizing a Bible verse from a list that's provided to them in prison. If several kids are being chased, any three kids can drop to their knees and pray, and the tempter has to flee.

There's no winning or losing in this game—it's just to teach the symbolism of the devil seeking out people to destroy (1 Peter 5:8), the power of praying together (Matthew 18:20), and the power God gives us to resist temptation so the devil will flee (James 4:7). You may want to wind up this game with a little talk or group discussion about temptation and what the kids learned. *Greg Sytsma*

REBEL STRIKE

All you need to create an awesome, space-theme game are the following:
- A ping-pong ball for each player—or anything soft, like rolled-up socks or Nerf balls
- Six rolls of toilet paper wrapped with packing tape (the tape will keep the rolls from unraveling, but allow the kids to see the toilet paper so they aren't afraid to get hit by it)
- Masking tape to mark the boundaries
- Six to eight hula hoops or masking tape circles on the floor. (Hula hoops add the challenge of a moving trail. As the kids run down the path, the

hoops are certain to get moved around.)
• One wiffle bat
• One wastebasket turned upside down with a large plastic cup sitting on top of it

The playing field can be almost any size, depending on the size of your group. A good-size playing field to start with is the length of a basketball court and 20 to 25 feet wide. Set up the playing field so it looks like the diagram below. Set a wastebasket with the plastic cup on top at one end of the field. This is the power source. Place the hoops one to two feet apart. For added difficulty you can increase the distance between the hoops with each round.

To track the teams' scores and help keep the game moving, you'll need to position adult leaders strategically. Place one near the power source to set the cup back on the wastebasket and realign the hoops before each team begins its attack. Place another leader at the end of each of the boundary lines to make sure no members of the Empire Forces step over the line during play. Another adult can be on TP duty, making sure each new attacker has a roll of toilet paper before beginning a run. Finally, someone should keep an eye on attackers and make sure they go to the end of the line when they're hit by ping-pong balls.

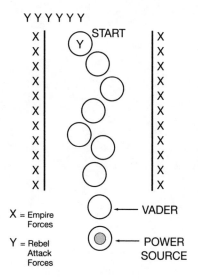

X = Empire Forces

Y = Rebel Attack Forces

Form teams of six to 10 players. Determine which team will be the Rebel Attack Force for the first round. As the first group lines up at the starting line, arm each team member with a roll of toilet paper.

All the players who aren't on the attack for that round will be the Empire Forces defending the power source, positioned around the perimeter of the playing field. Give each defender a ping-pong ball. Each defender is allowed to throw the ball only once during a round and cannot pick any ping-pong

ammunition off the floor to throw. It will take the Empire Forces a few rounds to develop a strategy of defense. Select one person from among the Empire Forces to act as Darth Vader for each round. Give that player a wiffle bat light saber to use to defend himself from inside Vader's hula hoop.

Each Rebel Attack Force will have two to four minutes, in relay style of play, to destroy the power source by knocking the cup off the wastebasket. Have someone time each round. The Attack Force team scores ten points whenever this happens— even if the cup is hit by a roll of toilet paper, accidentally whacked by Vader's light saber, or the wastebasket is somehow knocked over completely.

One by one, the Rebel Attack Force players will run through the hula hoops toward the power source—they can't step outside the hula hoops—and then try to throw their toilet paper past Vader so it will knock off the cup. And Vader uses the light saber to try to knock the toilet paper away from the power source.

Meanwhile, the Empire Forces are throwing their ping-pong balls at the runners. If a player is hit by a ping-pong ball, he has to return to the end of his team's line and let the next person go. If he makes it to Vader without being hit but also fails to knock off the cup, he returns to the back of the line to try again (running along the outside of the playing field). Players run through the course until the power source has been destroyed or until time's up for the team.

Attackers can go after the power source as often as possible in their team's two- to four-minute time limit.

Award 10 points to the Rebel Attack Force each time their team destroys the power source, and one point whenever a member of the Empire Forces steps over the line. Deduct one point from the Rebel Attack Force each time a player steps outside a hula hoop while running the course. No points are deducted for being hit by a ping-pong ball—the person just returns to the end of the line.

The only time a team can score points is when it's the Rebel Attack Force. The team of rebels with the most points at the end of the game can just sit back and relax as the evil opposing forces clean up all the ping-pong balls, toilet paper, and masking tape. *Doug Partin*

Receiving Line

This is a fun way for every member of a large group to meet the others. The first person introduces herself to the second person, and then stands next to the first person as a part of the receiving line. The third person introduces himself to the first person and the second person and then stands in line next to the second person. The following people go through the same procedure, until the last one has passed down the line. You can make it a competition between two groups, or just keep it going while music is playing. A great way to learn names!

Favorites

Have kids walk around until the leader yells out a favorite category, such as a color. At that point students yell out their favorite—blue, for example—and get in groups according to their favorites. Keep the game going as long as you want. Favorites can include color, season, food, sport, music group, clothing store, soda, Internet provider, et cetera. This is also a good way to divide the kids into small groups for another activity or discussion.

FOR SMALL GROUPS

Flexibility is the key here. While these games will work best in groups of thirty or less, most of them can be adapted for use in larger groups. And while some require a large indoor space, such as a fellowship hall or gymnasium, others can be played in a living room.

9-SQUARE

Nine-square is a fast-moving game that's great for nine to 20 players per court. To make the playing area, divide a 9' x 9' square into three-foot blocks and number them one through nine, with number one being the center block (see diagram).

This game is played like foursquare. Nine students take their places on the playing area, one person per square. The player in square number one serves the ball by bouncing it once inside his own square, then hitting it to one of the other eight. The player who receives the ball must let it bounce once before trying to hit it. A player can touch the ball before it bounces, but she must let it bounce before hitting it to another player. To block a hard-hit ball, a player should block the ball down so it bounces inside her square first and then hit it to another player.

Players try to get into the number-one square by ousting the players in front of them (players in squares with lower numbers than theirs) with difficult shots that result in misplayed balls. Ways of being eliminated include making an overhand hit, stepping outside a square with both feet, or hitting a

ball that lands on a line. Once a player is eliminated, he returns to the end of the line and everyone else moves up a square. As players reach the head of the line, they join the game on square number nine, which begins a new round.

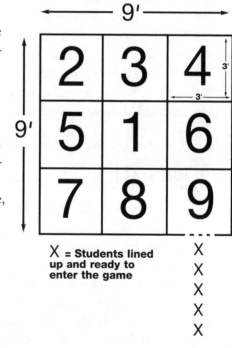

X = Students lined up and ready to enter the game

Play for a predetermined amount of time, or end the game when the student in the number-one square has defeated each of the rest of the players. *Gary Trotnic*

BIN BALL

After the youth group divides in half, students should number off and then stand in a large circle, with one complete set of numbers making up each half (see diagram). The order of the numbers isn't important, as long as each team makes up one side of the circle. Place two playground balls inside an empty trashcan in the center of the circle.

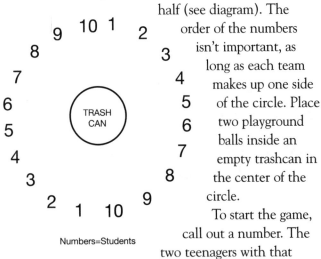

Numbers=Students

To start the game, call out a number. The two teenagers with that number should dash to the wastebasket to retrieve one of the balls. With balls in hand, the students run outside the circle (preferably through their vacant spots), take a lap around the rest of the players, and then hurry back to the middle. The first player to return a ball to the trashcan wins.

Call out a different number and start a race between two new students. Repeat the process as long as your kids have the energy to run in circles! *Troy Smith*

BLIND BALL

You need two blindfolds and a basketball-sized ball containing a bell or other noisy object. Blindfold two students and position them so they're facing each other from opposite ends of the playing area.

Kids will take turns rolling the ball toward each other as hard and fast as they can (a side-arm motion works the best), each one trying to aim it so the player at the other end of the room can't touch or stop the ball as it rolls past.

A point is scored whenever a player successfully sends the ball past her opponent. Set a scoring limit, then rotate other students into the game so they can take a roll against the current champion. *Jenny Shorter*

GREAT WIND-OFF

If you know a kid with a toy box full of self-propelled racecar toys (the ones you pull backward to wind and then let 'er rip), see if you can borrow a few for these two games.

Tape off a 12" x 12" square at one end of the room. Make a starting line about 20 feet from the taped-off area and give each player a racer toy. When you say, "Ready," all players should pull back their toys and wait for you to say, "Go!" before letting their toys take off across the floor.

Wherever their toys stop, players start over from that point, aim their toys toward the designated area, and wait for you to give the next signal. The first player to get the toy inside the square wins.

Or you can tape a line that's six to 10 feet away from the starting line. Everyone kneels at the starting line with their toys, waits for the signal, and then lets their toys go flying down the floor. The toy that stops the closest to the line without going over it wins. *Ken Lane*

RECORD ROLL

Still have a box of LPs in your garage? Take them out and give 'em another spin, so to speak. Tape off a finish line about 20 feet away from a designated starting point.

The students should kneel at the starting point and stand their circles of vinyl on edge, placing one finger on top to hold them steady before giving their records a good push toward the finish line. Everyone gets two rolls per round. Wherever a player's record stops becomes that person's new starting point from which to make a second attempt to reach the finish line.

Scoring can be done in a couple of ways. The winner can be the one whose record lands closest to the finish line without rolling over it. Or players can try to make their records land as close to the center of the finish line as possible. It's not as easy as it sounds. These records will follow some crazy paths as they roll across the floor. *Ken Lane*

Bucket Hats

You can play this game with your entire youth group or just ask for four or more contestants to compete in front of the rest of the group.

You'll need five or six two-liter plastic bottles and one old baseball cap per player, plus a jumbo-size bag of miniature marshmallows. To construct the bucket hats, cut the bottoms off the soda bottles so they're about four inches deep. Then staple six bottle bottoms (or however many will fit) around the brim of each baseball cap (see illustrations below).

Ask students to pair up and put on their bucket hats so the bills are pointed behind them. Then give each player 25 marshmallows as ammunition.

Partners should stand facing each other with eight feet between them as they attempt to toss the marshmallows into their teammates' buckets. Allow 30 seconds of play. After time runs out, add up the total number of marshmallows in each player's hat. The pair who catches the most mini-mallows between the two of them wins. *Len Cuthbert*

Duct-Tape Challenge

If you're stuck for game ideas and you have no props except some rolls of duct tape that were borrowed from the janitor's closet and never returned—you have the makings of a game! (Make sure no one cares about the walls you are about to abuse. Otherwise, your youth group's annual project for next year may be to repaint the gym or re-plaster the pastor's office. You know what—just don't do this in the pastor's office.)

Line up some low chairs or stools, one per team, near a wall in your youth room and leave two or

three feet of space between them. Divide your students into equal teams and ask them to each select a representative to stand on one of the chairs. Now give each team two rolls of duct tape.

Teams have five minutes to tape their representatives to the wall as quickly and securely as they can. Note: Don't tape the person's neck or head, just the limbs and torso. The first team to finish gets 10 bonus points.

Gently remove the chairs from underneath the contestants. Whoever stays taped to the wall the longest gets 10 points for his team. Obviously, the team with the most points wins.

If your contestants are very securely taped and boredom begins to set in, announce that the first person to get off the wall with no help will score a win for his or her team.

If you end up with a tie, your panel of judges could award or deduct points for things like "Neatest Tape Job," "Whiniest Contestant," "Worst Looking Patch of Wall" (after the tape is removed), and so on. *Curt Gibson*

Duct-Tape Engineers

Remember those Vacation Bible School crafts from summers past? This activity will create some new memories while your kids get some hands-on training in teamwork, creativity, and patience.

Groups of four sit in a circle on the floor. In the middle of each group, place a pile of craft supplies like scissors, markers, cotton balls, toothpicks, Scotch tape, newspaper, popsicle sticks, glitter, glue sticks, bric-a-brac, and pipe cleaners. Pass around rolls of duct or electrical tape and ask the students to help each other tape the hands they write with to the floor (a couple of pieces of tape across the wrist will be sufficient).

Now assign each group something to create with their supplies—animals, people, objects—and give them 15 minutes to work on it together, with only their remaining hands. When everyone is finished, let them untape their hands for the group presentations.

As each group shows their masterpiece to the rest of the students, the other kids should try to guess what each project is supposed to be. You can give prizes for the most recognizable creation, the most creative use of supplies, the best craftsmanship, and so on. *Scott Hundley*

PICK IT UP

Small teams of students choose one player to wrap from shoulders to ankles in masking or duct tape—sticky side out! While they're taking a couple of minutes to mummify their lucky volunteers, spread lots and lots of ripped sheets of paper all over the floor—the more paper the better and funnier the game will be!

When they're told to go, the mummified players must get down on the floor and roll around in the paper. The object is to pick up as much paper as they can by getting it stuck to their taped bodies. Give them about a minute of rolling time.

After time has run out, the rolling players' teammates should help them stand up and then start extracting the paper from the tape and counting pieces of paper. Watch players so they don't rip a piece of paper and count it as two! The team with the most paper stuck on their player wins. *Martha Martin*

HELP! I CUT MYSELF SHAVING

Give each team of four a glue stick and a roll of toilet paper. Three people on each team will race to use as much toilet paper as they can, by tearing off little pieces of TP and sticking them all over their teammate. You may wish to ask the teams to choose their representative *before* you explain what's going to happen to this unlucky, soon-to-be-sticky person.

After about three minutes, signal the end of the game and ask your panel of judges to vote for the best one—whoever is most completely covered in toilet paper. *Ken Lane*

GREEN EGGS AND HAM

Here's a new twist to an old favorite—Fruit Basket Upset. Ask the group to move their chairs into a circle, then take away one of them so you have one less chair than you have players. Have the person who is now without a chair stand in the center.

Instead of giving everyone fruit names, assign them repeating rhymes from the Dr. Seuss classic *Green Eggs and Ham*. For instance, they can be

boats, goats, trains, rain, trees, cars, foxes, boxes, and so on.

Now read *Green Eggs and Ham* out loud. When players hear you read their assigned names, they must leave their seats and find new ones. In the meantime, the player in the center tries to take any available seat and leave someone else to be "It." When you say the phrase "Sam I am" or "green eggs and ham," then *everybody* gets up to find a new seat. *Pat McGlone*

YOU'RE IT!

Make a circle of chairs with one fewer seat than you have players. Ask everyone to take a seat. The person who is left without a chair is now "It" and must stand in the middle. To begin the game, "It" asks the question, "Have you ever _____?" and fills in the blank with something she has actually done. Players who have done whatever she described must get up and move *at least* two chairs away from where they started to an empty chair.

Now there are two kinds of questions that "It" can ask. One is very specific, causing only a few people to get up. For example, "Have you ever stayed up until three o'clock in the morning talking about life, the universe, and everything else with your best friend?" The second type of question will make everyone get up and move. For example, "Have you ever tied your shoelaces?"

Once students are out of their chairs, "It" also tries to take a seat, leaving a new player to be "It" for the next round. *Carl Fuglein*

MOVE IT

Players wear nametags with their first names written on them in large letters. The group should pair off, except for one player who won't have a partner at first. Arrange the players' chairs in a large circle. One person in each pair must sit back in his chair with his feet firmly planted on the floor, while his partner stands behind him with her hands behind her back.

The person without a partner is also part of the circle, but he stands behind an empty chair. This lone player begins the game by calling the name of someone in the group. The person who's called tries to quickly get up and go sit in the empty chair. Meanwhile, that person's partner grabs for her shoulders to try to keep her in her seat.

If the seated player escapes to the empty chair, her old partner continues the game by calling a different player's name. But if the seated player cannot get away, then the player with the empty chair moves on and tries calling someone else. The rule is that if the person behind the chair grabs her partner's shoulders, the partner is caught. We're not looking for wrestling matches between partners here.

It doesn't matter if there are duplicate names in the group. That just makes it more exciting as everyone with that name goes for the empty chair. *The Community Presbyterian Church of Clarendon Hills, Illinois*

POOL-NOODLE NAMES

Everyone but one player sits in a circle. The player in the center holds half a foam pool noodle.

One person starts by saying her name, followed by the name of another player in the circle. The person in the middle tries to bop the second player gently on the head before she can say her name and name another player. If he succeeds, he gets to relinquish the pool noodle and take a seat in that player's chair.

The player who's about to sit down begins the next round of play by saying his name followed by someone else's. However, he must do it before sitting down. If he forgets and sits in the chair before restarting the game, he must go back to the middle of the circle and wait for his next opportunity to bop someone. If he succeeds, the person he names must say her name and the name of another person.

If your group catches on quickly, you can vary it a little by having the players make up silly names for themselves. Then everyone, including the player in the middle, must remember the players' new names for the remainder of the game. *Jonathan Dixon*

WHO WANTS TO BE A TEENAGER?

This game is played the same as *Who Wants to Be a Millionaire?* but you ask your students and parents to write some multiple-choice questions that pertain to the culture and interests of their own generation.

Teenage contestants sitting in the "hot seat" are asked questions that were written by the parents.

When it's the parents' turn to answer, they receive questions written by the students.

A variation is that team members take turns sitting in the hot seat during a round of the game. So each player answers one question before letting someone else take the seat. This continues until someone answers incorrectly, and then it's the other team's turn to answer questions as long as they can.

Once the three lifelines have been used by three players, they're lost to the whole team until the next round. Is that your final answer? *Michael Welter*

WHO WANTS TO BE A BIBLE SCHOLAR?

To prepare, choose eight Bible questions (per round of the game) ahead of time, ranging in difficulty from easy to very challenging. Specify four answers to each question, one of which is right. Decide on eight prizes that fit the difficulty of the questions. As you're choosing prizes, remember that if someone gets up to question seven, she gets the prize for question seven—but doesn't get the prizes for questions one through six. Last, set up two chairs facing each other and place a Bible on one of them (yours).

When your group arrives, pass out Bibles if your kids don't come with them, and hold a Sword Draw contest where you read a Scripture and the first person to stand up and read it wins. (No electronic devices allowed!) The winner of this contest is your first contestant on *Who Wants to Be a Bible Scholar?* Explain that the contestant gets three lifelines: 50/50 (where two wrong answers out of the four choices are eliminated), ask a friend, and 30-second Bible search. Tell the group about the prizes (but don't say what they are!).

Now sit in the Bible chair and have your contestant sit in the other. If you want, play some suspense-type music in the background after reading each question.

You can play as many rounds of this as you want to include more students. If you do, plan more prizes. *Kurt Halvorsen*

WALK A MILE IN THEIR SHOES (A GAME SHOW FOR PARENTS)

Make some initial arrangements and invite eight to 10 parents to be contestants on a "Family Feud" kind of show about the lives of teenagers today.

Divide your students into planning teams and assign different tasks to each group, such as making up the survey questions (all about teen interests). For example, "Name a top 10 band that teenagers listen to." "Name the top three pressures teenagers feel today." "Name the top 10 worries of a teenager." "Name six things teenagers do to get ready for the prom." "Name the top 10 things teenagers want from their parents."

Ask another group to design the set, find good theme music to play, make applause signs—all the stuff that will add realism to the atmosphere of the show. A third group could work together to create the answer board using poster board or a PowerPoint program and a projector. Other groups can write and videotape segments to be used as commercial breaks during the game show. You'll also need to choose someone—perhaps a staff member or a student with lots of charisma—to be the host.

Invite all the kids' parents to come and enjoy the show. The important thing is that the parents will learn more about their teenagers, while the generations have an evening of fun together. *Anne Scott*

BEST SEAT IN THE HOUSE

When a couple of your students deserve some special treatment or a little TLC, let them choose a couple of friends to hang out with them in the "Best Seat in the House," either during youth group or after the meeting has wrapped up.

It doesn't take much effort to create the atmosphere of a comfortable living room somewhere in your youth room. With just a couch, a chair (use inflatable furniture—it's easier to store), a table, and a lamp set up on a platform, those lucky students will have all the comforts of home! You might even hook up a video game system to a big screen TV and supply a cooler full of drinks and snacks to enhance the experience.

You can be as elaborate or as simple as you like

with the accommodations, but the point is to make a student feel special and rewarded for good attendance, inviting lots of unchurched friends to youth events, or other positive behaviors you wish to encourage among your students. *Dan Atchison*

TOM AND JERRY

Players sit on chairs in a circle. Use a small pillow or stuffed animal as "Jerry" (that loveable cartoon mouse) and two big pillows for the "Toms" (his feline predator). The goal is to try to eliminate the other players. The only way to do this is to nail the player who's holding Jerry with one of the Toms.

Jerry must be passed from player to player—not thrown. However, Toms can be picked up and thrown by anyone. Players who are tagged out remain where they are, but turn their chairs around so they face outside the circle. As players are removed from the game, it will become harder to hand Jerry off. If a player can't easily hand Jerry to another player, she can walk over—walk!—and deliver it to another student. No throwing the mouse!

The excitement increases as players desperately try to get rid of Jerry while Toms are flying through the air. The last person in the circle wins. *Michl Kohl*

GLADIATOR SOCKS

Take two old but clean knee-high gym socks and stuff each sock with another sock. Mark off a 10" x 10" square with masking tape. The contestants must remain within these boundaries during the game.

Gladiators compete by swinging their war socks at one another, each trying to land the first blow (provide goggles for the players), and a referee decides who struck first. Tournament play works well, with the winner moving on to fight again. Or you could play the best two out of three rounds. *Eric D. Robinson*

HOSE HEAD FEDERATION CHALLENGE

Cut the legs off a pair of pantyhose. Fill the toe of each leg with flour and secure a rubber band around the ankle area to keep the flour inside the toe. Use masking tape or duct tape to mark off a boxing ring on the floor of your meeting room and tape the letters *HHF*, for "Hose Head Federation," in the center of the ring.

Choose two competitors and designate one player as the champ and the other as the challenger. When the students place the stockings over their heads, the toes full of flour should hang down to the gladiators' waists.

Ring a bell to start the match. Now the students begin moving their heads so the flour-filled nylons will swing in circles as they try to hit their opponents with them. It's obvious when hits are scored because of the marks made by the flour. The length of each round can vary.

The student with the fewest flour marks at the end of a round is named the new champion and remains in the ring to take on the next challenger. Let the tournament continue until one student is proven the biggest Hose Head in the world!

AUSTRALIAN PILLOW BOXING

Before the event, take four 1" x 6" x 6' boards and nail them onto a 2' x 2' piece of plywood to form an X (see diagram below). Place the X in the center of the room and a circle of orange safety cones around the perimeter of the playing area for safety. If you like a little more drama, cover the windows and rig up a spotlight directly above the center of the boards.

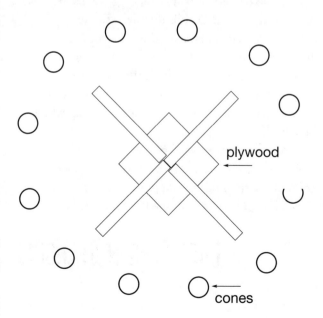

plywood

cones

Divide your teenagers into four teams and give each team a pillow. When you ask four contestants to come forward, each group should send a representative to stand on one of the four boards that make the X. It's wiser and safer to try to match opponents of equal size or ability by calling out the desired age and gender of the four players needed for each round. This will help prevent a senior guy from clobbering a freshman girl during the game.

A key element that will make or break this game is the cheering of the spectators. Tell the students that points will be awarded to their teams for enthusiastic cheering. The louder and more creative it is, the more points their team will receive.

When the four competitors are in position with their pillows in hand, explain that when the whistle blows they should try to knock their three opponents off the boards. Players may not touch their opponents' boards or the floor with any part of their body or pillow to do this.

If you choose to use the spotlight, turn it on now and turn off all the other lights. Crank up the *Rocky* soundtrack, blow the whistle, and let the fun begin! Play as many rounds as you can so all the kids who want to participate have a chance to do so. With kids screaming from all sides and the spotlight focusing all eyes on the center ring, this is an intense event that kids will rave about for weeks. *Rob Baird*

WALLOP

You need a balance beam, mats to put under the beam, and some heavy-duty pillows. If you don't have a balance beam, a 4" x 4" piece of wood attached to shorter 4" x 4" pieces on both ends will do. Place a piece of duct tape across the center of the balance beam and two more pieces about 18 inches away on either side. (See illustration on page 38.)

Divide the students into teams of four or five for this tournament. The first two teams to compete should line up on the beam, facing in opposite directions. In other words, eight to 10 people should be standing on the beam at one time and neither team should be watching their hitter. The object is to knock your opponent's entire team off the beam— one at a time.

To begin the game, the hitters (the two players at the very center of the beam) are given pillows and directions to begin walloping each other. However, they're only allowed to hit their opponents on the back and behind. No headshots or hitting below the behind are allowed. In addition, the hitters must keep their feet within their own 18-inch areas of the beam at all times. When one of the hitters falls off, the next person in line becomes the hitter. And if someone falls off the beam before getting a chance to be the hitter, that person must stay off.

You may wish to impose a 30-second time limit for each set of hitters, just in case both are able to stay on the beam. After 30 seconds are up, call a draw and both hitters must get off the beam and let the next hitters have a turn. This game is a riot to watch and to play! *Jeff Hicks*

Hot Chocolate Scramble

Groups of six to eight students will compete to see who will be the first to finish eating a king-size candy bar. Have the kids sit around a table or in a circle on the floor. Then place a wrapped candy bar, a pair of dice, a plastic knife and fork, and a set of winter outerwear (gloves, hat, and scarf) in the center of each group.

The oldest person in the circle gets to roll the dice first. If he rolls doubles, he may start eating the candy bar—but there's a catch. He has to put on the gloves, scarf, and hat, run around the circle once, try to unwrap the candy bar while wearing the gloves,

and *then* eat the candy bar—using the knife and fork to cut it into one-inch pieces.

Meanwhile, the rest of the players continue to take turns rolling the dice. If someone else rolls doubles, the first player must leave the candy, costume, and eating utensils where they are and return to his seat. The second player goes through the same routine as the first, also trying to eat the candy before another player rolls doubles.

The game ends when the candy bars are finally eaten. *Gwyn Baker and Tedd Brent*

Gloves Gift Frenzy

You need a pretty good prize to start with. Pick something your kids will enjoy, like a CD, a book, a bag of candy, or a video. It also helps if it's a small gift because you're going to do a lot of wrapping. They're really going to have to work for this one!

Wrap the gift as though you're an ancient Egyptian undertaker, but without the spices and formaldehyde. Use layers and layers of various types of wrapping supplies: Scotch tape, masking tape, duct tape, newspaper, plastic bags, boxes inside boxes, more wrapping paper, old towels, and so forth. Get creative with the wrapping and make it a real pain to get into, yet still make it look really nice on the outside.

To start, everyone sits in a circle around the gift and a pair of heavy mittens. A leader walks around with a cake pan and a pair of dice, giving each kid a turn to roll. If a player rolls doubles, she runs to the middle of the circle, puts on the mittens, and starts unwrapping the present. She keeps at it until someone else rolls doubles, at which time she stops, removes the mittens, and returns to her spot in the circle, leaving the new contestant to take up where she left off.

The game continues this way with layer after layer being slowly peeled away until the kid who removes the final bit of wrapping is declared the winner and gets to take home the prize. *Marshall Allen*

Last Person Standing

Twenty-four students can play this game at one time. Lay out a playing grid with masking tape, made up of four-foot by four-foot squares as shown on page 40.

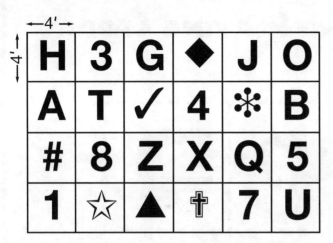

Photocopy **Last Person Standing Playing Cards** (page 40) and cut the cards apart. Each player will wear a flag football belt with two flags (flag color doesn't matter).

Begin by asking the players to stand one in each square. When you say, "Go!" each player moves to another square. Whenever players are on the move, they're allowed to go after each other's flags. If a player's flag is pulled, he's out and should sit down outside the playing field. And any time two or more players stop in the same square, they should try to pull each other's flags. The first one to lose a flag is out.

Once players are standing in their new squares, someone draws a symbol card from the deck. The square that matches the drawn symbol is off limits for the rest of the game, and whoever is standing on that square is also eliminated. For the duration of the game, players will need to remember which squares are out. If later in the game someone should happen to stop in a square that's considered out of play, that person will be sitting on the sidelines with the rest of the ousted players.

The game continues until only one player remains, and the last person standing is the winner.

Rod Nielsen

PITS

Despite its complicated nature, this has proven to be a worthy game, both as a discussion starter and just for fun. To play you'll need a large room with plenty of floor space. You also need to create some place markers. These should be identical in appearance on one side, but on the other write the words SAFE SPOT or YOU ARE IN A PIT. A sheet of 8½ x 11 cardstock

paper makes a fine place marker and can be used several times before it needs to be replaced. (But if this game becomes a favorite in your group, it would be worth the money to invest in some 12-inch round cardboard disks, like the kind bakers use to decorate cakes.) To begin with, about 40 percent of the cards should be pits and the other 60 percent safe spots. The ratio of pits to safe spots can vary, but you may wish to learn the game with a smaller percentage of pits at first.

To set up the game, shuffle all the markers to generate a random field of play and ensure that every game will be different. Place markers face down on the floor in a rectangular pattern of five columns and six rows (this pattern is variable). Markers must be two to three feet apart and arranged in an orderly pattern so legal moves will be obvious to the appointed referees. Choose one side of the field to be the starting row and the other end as the exit row. You may also choose to designate just one space as the exit marker.

The game works best with five to 10 players or else teams of this size may compete against each other. Players stand near the markers in the starting row and begin by turning the markers over. If a flipped marker is a safe spot, then that player may stand on it and wait to proceed. But if the marker is a pit, the person must immediately sit down because she's now stuck in a pit. Only the players who are

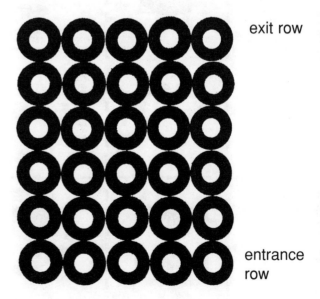

exit row

entrance row

standard play field

LAST PERSON STANDING PLAYING CARDS

Copy this page onto a sheet of cardstock paper and cut the squares apart to make a deck of cards.

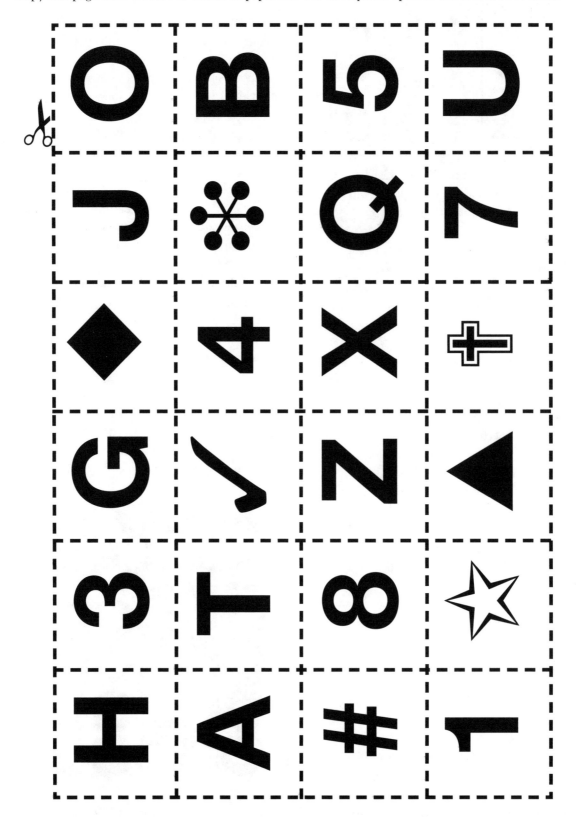

standing on safe spots may continue playing by each flipping over an adjacent marker. And diagonal moves are not permitted in this particular playing field (see the variations described below). Touching a marker in any way is a commitment to move to that space. No exceptions!

Players in pits aren't doomed to remain there for the rest of the game—there are two ways they can return to the action and another way they can help their teammates avoid their same fate:

1. Rescue: Two players may join together in one adjacent safe spot and pull a player out of a pit, but the three must now link arms and stay together for the duration of the game. Where one goes, the other two must go unless they fall into a pit together. Any threesome that falls into a pit is no longer obligated to remain together.

2. Escape: Two players in a pit may discharge a third player by pushing him out of the pit. If a threesome falls into a pit, they must agree on who will leave. Then that player may move to either an adjacent space that has been previously revealed as a safe spot or an unrevealed space marker. And if the unknown marker should reveal a safe spot, that discharged player may now continue to play alone. However, if the space is a pit, that player is stuck alone in the adjacent pit.

3. Bridge: Two players in a pit can agree to serve as a bridge for other players to cross to an adjacent safe spot. The bridge option simply saves time when it's decided that going through a pit is the best route for the group.

Directions for getting out of a pit should be written on the back of each pit marker so you don't have to explain how to get out of the pit six dozen times during the game. **Directions for Leaving a Pit** can be found on page 42 for you to photocopy. It might be helpful to draw some stick figures, like the examples below, to visibly represent these three options for your players.

Once players reach the exit row and leave the field of play, they may not return. When all players either have exited safely or remain stuck in the pits, the game is over.

Here are some variations to the game you can try:

• **Silent Pits.** Don't allow any verbal communication during the game. Nonverbal cues are essential for anyone to survive.

• **Altered Fields of Play.** Try different field patterns like a narrower and longer field or a forked path.

• **Extra Pits.** The percentage of pits in a field can be increased for greater challenge. You can even choose to concentrate pits in one or more areas, like the entire starting row!

• **Limited Pathways.** Another idea is to use sidewalk chalk or masking tape to draw some predetermined paths between field markers for players to follow.

• **Pit Race.** Set the markers in a spiral pattern with connecting lines drawn or taped on the floor. Two groups can compete in a race to the center.

• **Treasure Pits.** Place Post-It notes on the undersides of random markers to designate the location of treasure. Teams can compete, or let the students form their own alliances during the game. The winner(s) must safely exit the field *with* the treasure in order to get the grand prize. For an added twist, place the treasure in a pit and see what happens! *Dale Nixon*

NEWSPAPER QUIZ

Look through some newspapers and find 10 or more pieces of information. You can use articles, classifieds, advertisements, headlines, or any other section of the paper. Organize the information into a list that contains 10 to 20 questions. For example, if you

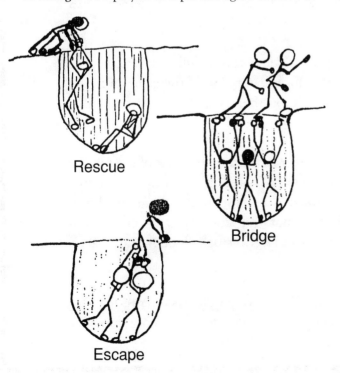

Rescue

Bridge

Escape

Directions for Leaving a Pit

Once a player is in the pit, there are only two ways to get out and one way to help teammates avoid the same fate:

1. Rescue: Two players may join together in one adjacent safe spot and pull a player out of a pit, but the three must now link arms and stay together for the duration of the game. Where one goes, the other two must go unless they fall into a pit together. Any threesome that falls into a pit is no longer obligated to remain together.

2. Escape: Two players in a pit may discharge a third player by pushing him out of the pit. If a threesome falls into a pit, they must agree on who will leave. Then that player may move to either an adjacent space that has been previously revealed as a safe spot or an unrevealed space marker. And if the unknown marker should reveal a safe spot, that discharged player may now continue to play alone. However, if the space is a pit, that player is stuck alone in the adjacent pit.

3. Bridge: Two players in a pit can agree to serve as a bridge for other players to cross to an adjacent safe spot. The bridge option simply saves time when it's decided that going through a pit is the best route for the group.

- -

Directions for Leaving a Pit

Once a player is in the pit, there are only two ways to get out and one way to help teammates avoid the same fate:

1. Rescue: Two players may join together in one adjacent safe spot and pull a player out of a pit, but the three must now link arms and stay together for the duration of the game. Where one goes, the other two must go unless they fall into a pit together. Any threesome that falls into a pit is no longer obligated to remain together.

2. Escape: Two players in a pit may discharge a third player by pushing him out of the pit. If a threesome falls into a pit, they must agree on who will leave. Then that player may move to either an adjacent space that has been previously revealed as a safe spot or an unrevealed space marker. And if the unknown marker should reveal a safe spot, that discharged player may now continue to play alone. However, if the space is a pit, that player is stuck alone in the adjacent pit.

3. Bridge: Two players in a pit can agree to serve as a bridge for other players to cross to an adjacent safe spot. The bridge option simply saves time when it's decided that going through a pit is the best route for the group.

see an advertisement for the new Ford Mustang at Joe's Lot-a-Cars, you might ask, "How much does a new Ford Mustang at Joe's Lot-a-Cars cost?"

Here's a list of sample questions to give you some more ideas.

1. How much does a 1998 Suburban cost at Schmidt's Chevrolet?
2. Fill in the blank: "You'll save up to ___ percent at the Bargain Place this Saturday."
3. How fast was Jon Smith going when police pulled him over this Saturday?
4. What is the name of the new drug being tested for cancer prevention?
5. According to Dr. Houston, what is the leading cause of hair loss in men over 50?
6. Who won the soccer game between the Highland Bulldogs and the Greenville Comets?
7. What show is on PBS channel 9 this Wednesday at 7:00 am?
8. What color tie was Bill Clinton wearing when he addressed the National Science Committee?
9. What is the estimated low temperature for this Tuesday night?
10. What date does construction begin on the Poplar Street Bridge?
11. What was the cause of death for Eleanor Smith this past weekend?
12. What kid's toy prize is being featured this month at Joe's Burger Barn?
13. How much do the cheapest tickets cost for the Dave Matthews concert this Thursday at the Kiel Center?
14. When is the new Taco Bell opening in Greenville?
15. What event is taking place this week on Governor Bond Lake?
16. Fill in the blank: "There's nothing quite like a _____ from Albert's cafe."
17. Name the law firm that is representing alleged crime boss Antonio Fonzarelli.
18. What new store will be coming to the Northwood Mall in January?
19. What is the estimated cost for restoring the City Hall building?
20. Which member of our youth group is featured in the Lifestyle section?

Divide your group into even teams of two to four players and give each team a stack of large newspapers, like the Sunday edition of the *New York Times*, *Los Angeles Times*, or *Chicago Tribune*. Every stack should contain identical copies of the same newspapers.

Read the first question out loud to the group. The first team to shout out the correct response gets a point. After this trial run, pick up the pace by throwing out several questions at a time. Maintaining a fast pace will keep the students more involved. The team with the most points at the end should be given the coveted Nose for News Award —travel-size packets of Kleenex. *Brian Morgan*

TEAR 'N' SPELL

There are three rounds to this game. You can use them all together as an interactive way to introduce the night's lesson, review a prior lesson, or even promote an upcoming youth event. You'll need newspapers, glue sticks, and a roll of butcher paper or newsprint for the students to share. Tape large sheets of butcher paper on the walls and set up workstations at each piece of butcher paper, enough to comfortably accommodate all the students in your youth group. Place a stack of newspapers and a glue stick or two at each station.

The first round could be considered a trial run during which each student plays alone. Players will race to try to find the letters or combinations of letters to spell their first and last names. They should tear the letters by hand and then glue them onto the paper.

The next game can be played individually or in teams of two or more (use larger teams for larger groups). The leader calls out relevant or key words from a current Bible study, a lesson series, or an announcement about an upcoming youth group event like a retreat or missions trip. Then each person or team tries to find the letters to spell out those words, tears them out, and attaches them to the paper.

Finally, the same teams should compete to be the first to find and create a given sentence. Again, it could be relevant to a current Bible study, lesson series, or youth event.

After the last two rounds, award teams first, second, and third place in categories like speed, neatness in tearing and gluing, creativity, the largest group of letters or words found in the newspaper, and so on. *Len Cuthbert*

TIC TAC PREACH

Here's a chance to see how well your students follow current events while testing their ability to speak well under pressure. You could use this activity as a lead-in for the topic of good witnessing—why Christians should always be prepared to explain their faith and do it in a competent way.

Before the game, go through a local newspaper and write down 20 local, national, or global current event issues. Tape a large Tic Tac Toe board at the front of your room and choose a panel of judges from your adult volunteers. Now split the group into two teams—guys versus girls, upperclassmen versus underclassmen, etc.—and choose one team to be the Xs and the other to be the Os.

Call a representative from each team to the front. Give representatives a topic and five to 10 seconds to form an opinion about it. Based on whether or not each player's statement is coherent or articulate—not necessarily "right"—the panel of judges then gives the speaker thumbs up or thumbs down! The player with the majority of thumbs-up votes from the judges gets to place her team's symbol (an X or an O) on the board. Ask two more players to come forward, and give them a new issue to talk about. The first team to get a line of Xs or Os wins the round. *John Wilkinson*

PEOPLE-SENTENCE BOGGLE

Write words on individual sheets of paper, one word per sheet and one sheet per player. Below is a suggested list of words you can use, but feel free to add to it. Divide your group into at least two teams and have each team choose a captain. You need one complete set of words for each team, so make sure each team captain gets enough sheets of paper for himself and all teammates.

Captains should give each of their teammates a sheet of paper with a word written on it, but don't

A (2)	**Man**
And (2)	**Me**
Any	**Off**
Are	**Old**
Around	**On**
Bad	**Out**
Beast	**Over**
Boy	**Show**
Can	**Soft**
Clean	**Some**
Cold	**The (2)**
Eye	**Them**
Face	**Them (2)**
Foot	**This**
From	**Throw**
Girl	**Time**
Good	**To**
Her	**Under**
Him	**Us**
In	**What**
Is (2)	**When**
It (2)	**Which**
Lady	**Will**
Lap	**Work**

let anyone look yet. Once everyone is holding a word, yell, "Start!" Now the teams have two minutes to study their words and come up with a sentence that uses some of them. Each word used is worth five points, so the more words a team uses, the better its score.

Team captains should organize their people and help them line up in the proper order. When time is up, one person can read the team's sentence aloud or the team members, in turn, can say their words aloud.

For the next round, teams can choose new captains and go again if they like, or you can give them a whole new set of words to try. *Denise Lutterman*

GOO WHO?

This fun game takes a bit of preparation and some 21st-century technology. You need a computer,

Kai's Power Goo morphing software program, and a projector if your group is large. Scan some pictures of your students and leaders using *Kai's Power Goo*. Morph the pictures before your meeting a step at a time until they can't be identified easily.

Divide your teens into teams. Show them a morphed picture, and let them work together to figure out the identity. Occasionally reverse the gooing process a step at a time until one of the teams identifies the subject of the picture. Go slowly enough to foster guesses. If you can't set your group around the monitor or projection screen, you'll need to print a series of each picture.

You can set up your own rules about whether you want kids to be called on before answering and whether you want to establish a winner-takes-all or a gradually decreasing point system. *Dan Anthony*

SOUND BYTES

From the Internet, download a variety of sound clips from movies, television shows, cartoons, and so forth. Divide your students into teams of eight to 10. Each team should choose a runner and a backup runner for each round of play, someone who'll run to the front of the room to share the team's response.

Play the sound clips on your computer, holding a microphone next to the speaker so everyone can hear. The first runner to reach you is given a chance to name either the speaker or the origin of the clip (for example, what movie or television show it's from). If the first runner answers incorrectly, then the backup runner is given a chance to answer. Award one point for each correct answer. Give the winning team a round of applause. *Eddie Mullins*

PAPER ZAP

Ever seen "Sticky Hands"—those long, skinny, sticky products that act like frog tongues? A Sticky Hand is a rubber toy that can be snapped (like you'd snap a towel at someone) several feet away from you until it sticks to something. Then, with just a flick of the wrist, you can make it snap back with the desired object attached. You can get them at many toy or dollar stores, Wal-Mart, or even from the Oriental Trading Company and sometimes bubble gum vending machines. Before you play, buy enough

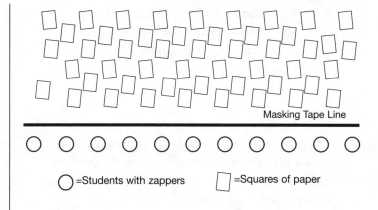

Masking Tape Line

◯ =Students with zappers   ▢ =Squares of paper

Sticky Hands so you have one per player (about 10 students can play at a time without too much chaos). Create about 100 squares of paper with a different point value written on each one. Each slip can be worth five, 10, 15, or 25 points, but only a few should be worth 25.

To play the game, put down a line of masking tape that players cannot cross during the game. Randomly spread out the paper squares face down on the floor on just one side of the line. Ask the players to line up on the opposite side and distribute the zappers. When you say, "Go!" they should "slap and snap" as many squares as they can. After all the paper has been picked up, players should total their points to determine the winner. *Bret Luallen*

HUNGRY, HUNGRY HIGH SCHOOLERS

If you've ever played the game "Hungry Hungry Hippos," you'll have no trouble picturing the setup for this one. You need one hula hoop and a bag of lightweight marbles for every four players, plus a Sticky Hand (see Paper Zap for information) for each competitor.

Put the hula hoops on the floor and have four players sit around each hoop about three feet away from the edge. Give each player a Sticky Hand and release a bag of marbles inside the hoop. Players stick and pull as many marbles as they can out of the circle until the hoop is empty. No moving the hoop! The player with the most marbles wins. *Jamie McDaniel*

STICK THE TAIL

Try this new variation of an old birthday party game.

45

Instead of a cartoon drawing of a donkey, use a poster of a famous person. (You may want to laminate it first so it won't get destroyed.) Or create your own picture by photocopying a drawing or piece of clip art onto a sheet of transparency, placing it on an overhead projector, and tracing the picture onto a large sheet of paper taped to the wall. Buy some stickers and be creative about your choices. If you have a poster of the current heart throb, for example, you can get stickers of big, red lips that the contestants can try to stick on.

Before the game begins, ask players to write their names or initials on their stickers so you can easily identify the winner at the end. Blindfold your first contestant, have her turn in a circle a few times, and then nudge her in the direction of the poster. Whoever gets a sticker closest to the designated target area on the poster can claim it as the prize. *Brian Moyer*

HUMAN PIÑATA

Fill your favorite volunteer staff person's pockets (or have him hold plastic grocery sacks while you fill them) with candy and other prizes. Dangle him from the ceiling with a pulley apparatus or a rock-climbing rope.

Choose some volunteers from the crowd, blindfold them, and then give each one a foam pool noodle, a Nerf bat, or anything softer than a Louisville Slugger to swing at the "piñata." Before her turn, spin each contestant in a circle and give her up to a minute to try to find the swinging staff member overhead. The spectators can shout out instructions, if necessary, to help each player try to locate the human piñata. After being hit a few times, but completely at his own discretion, the leader is free to throw down the candy and other loot for all to enjoy. *Chris Milbrath*

BIBLE BULL'S-EYE

Write out two Bible verses on index cards, placing only one or two words on each card. Tape the cards face down and in the proper order on a bulletin board. You can either use two bulletin boards, one for each team, or divide a very large bulletin board in half and tape one verse to each side. Place a line on the floor 10 feet away from the target (bulletin board). Students must stand behind this line during the game.

The teams should line up single file behind the throwing line directly across from the bulletin board. Teams will take turns throwing, and each player is allowed to throw three darts per turn (unless someone hits a card on the first or second throw—then that person is done for that turn). Obviously, strict rules should be enforced as to when and where the darts are thrown. In other words, do not throw the darts when the youth leader is standing in front of the board.

Every time a card is hit with a dart, turn it over and give that team a chance to guess what their verse says. If they answer correctly, they win. If not, that player goes to the end of the line and the first person in the next line gets three throws at his team's cards. Continue playing this way until a team correctly guesses their verse (think "Wheel of Fortune" here).

After one team wins, turn over all the cards on both bulletin boards so the verses can be read aloud. This is a great way to introduce a Bible verse before a lesson or study.

BIBLE SQUARES

Write 12 different names of books of the Bible on 12 pieces of poster board, one book per board. Tape the poster board to the floor to form a grid sized three rows by four columns (see diagram). Ahead of time, prepare a list of questions about those 12 books of the Bible, such as "What is the first book in the Bible?" or "What book tells the story of Noah?"

GENESIS	MATTHEW	HOSEA	REVELATION
1 KINGS	PSALMS	MICAH	1 TIMOTHY
ACTS	SONG OF SOLOMON	JUDGES	RUTH

Divide your group into two teams and make sure the students have access to several Bibles. One team goes first and chooses a representative to stand on the grid. Put one minute on the timer and ask the first question. Team members should work together to come up with an answer they can all agree on and then they tell their teammate where to stand on the grid. After you accept or reject their response, ask the next question. The players need to work fast because they only get a minute to answer as many questions as they can in each round. After time is up, the next team gets a minute. Continue to alternate players from the teams until you run out of questions.

Every right answer is worth 100 points, and the team with the most points wins. *Stacy Goebel*

FOLLOWING HIS FOOTSTEPS

Most youth group students, even non-Christian ones, are familiar with the basic idea behind the WWJD? movement with its bumper stickers and bracelets. But do they *really* know what Jesus did in different situations? The purpose of this game is to have fun and build community, while exploring the Bible and learning more about some of the choices Jesus made.

Make footprint shapes and tape single-color "foot paths" using different colors of construction paper—one color footprint for each route—throughout the room or church. Get creative—stick them on walls, have the trails lead into bathrooms, put them on toilet lids, even have them lead into the refrigerator in the church kitchen!

Create some stations along each path. The total number of stations you use will depend on how much time you have to play the game, but make at least four along each footpath. Each station will contain a card that gives the location of a Bible passage that talks about something Jesus said or did. Some suggested Scripture passages you can use are Matthew 5:14-16 (you could post this one on a light switch plate), Matthew 8:23-27; Matthew 14:22-32; Matthew 15:32-38; and Matthew 16:24.

Choose teams, one for each color of footprints. Give each team a clipboard with a copy of **Following His Footsteps** (page 48) and a pen or pencil attached to it. Teams can use these sheets to make notes and write down their answers as they go along. Encourage them to make notes, as each group will be asked to share their findings at the end of the game. Now assign each team a colored footpath to follow and send them on their way.

Every time a team stops at a station, they should look up the passage of Scripture listed on the card, read it, and then work together to discuss and answer the questions on their sheet. This should be done for every passage they come across along their journey.

After all the teams have returned to the starting point, give them the opportunity to share what they learned about what Jesus did and what they can do today if they follow his example. *Danielle Parish*

APPLIANCE-BOX SOCCER

Get some large cardboard boxes—the kind that once held large appliances like refrigerators, washing machines, or freezers—not microwaves or portable televisions. Cut holes in the boxes for arms and legs, and provide face-sized cutouts here and there for sticking faces out and being able to see. Set up the playing area like a soccer field, including a center-

Following His Footsteps

Pray with your team before you begin the journey.

Whenever you find a Scripture card at one of the stations along your path, stop. Read the passage aloud in your group. Then ask someone to take notes from your team's discussion of the following questions. Repeat these steps for every passage of Scripture you encounter along the way. Take turns reading the verses and answering the questions about them.

1. Summarize the verses.

2. What happened or what is being taught?

3. What can you do today to follow the example Jesus set for us back then?

Station 1	Station 2
Station 3	**Station 4**
Station 5	**Station 6**

line and goal at both ends.

Situate a box over each group of two or three kids, letting them figure out whose limbs go through which holes and whose face goes in which cutout, then position the players on the field. They must have a limb sticking out of every hole in the box and a face in every cutout! Put the soccer ball in motion with the beginning face-off and let 'em go for it! It's hilarious to watch because the kids can't see the ball when it's too close to them, which makes it hard to kick the ball. At some point your students will probably trip over each other and fall down in a heap, so have your video camera ready.

Recycle this fancy cardboard game gear by cutting new holes in different places and trying a rousing game of appliance-box baseball or volleyball.

Brandon Hill

BOX BLITZ

If you've gone to all the trouble to get some large cardboard boxes for **Appliance-Box Soccer** (page 47), then maybe you'd like to explore some more uses for them before they end up at the recycling center.

First cut off the short ends of the boxes so you're left with cardboard tubes. Now try any or all of these ideas:

• **Box Shoot.** Lay the boxes on their sides and have even teams (as many teams as you have boxes) line up single file about five feet away from the openings. Teams compete relay-style to see how many kids they can send through their boxes in 60 seconds.

• **Leap Box.** Form two teams of students. Lay all the boxes out in two rows—on their sides and end to end. Each team chooses five members to crawl into the row of boxes as fast as they can. After all five are inside, their teammates move the first boxes in each row to the other end of the line, leapfrog style. This enables the five crawlers to continue moving forward without touching the ground. The first team to cross the finish line at the other end of the room wins.

• **Kickboxing.** Form as many teams as you like. Players on each team line up and lie down side by side in a long row. Have adult volunteers help place a box on top of the first person in each line. When you give the signal, each team must pass their box

down the line using only their feet. First team to get their box to the end of the line without using their hands or arms wins.

• **Vertical Blind Relay.** Two teams of students compete in this relay race. Have the teams line up single file at one end of the room. At the other end, place two orange safety cones, folding chairs, or trashcans directly across from where the teams are lined up. Have four students from each team stand together in a clump, and then drop a box over them. The bottom of the box should come to about their thighs. The players inside the boxes should all help to hold the box so it remains at this level during the game.

Players can't put their faces in the cutouts left from the previous game so it'll be hard for them to see, so one of their teammates should be asked to run alongside and give directions during the race. Each box full of students must run to the other end of the room, circle their cone, chair, or trashcan, and then run back to their team. They should quickly pass the box to the next four students so they can go. The first team to finish wins.

• **Roll-a-Box.** Create a starting line and make a long row of boxes lying end to end on their sides. One person lies down inside each box, and three other students kneel beside each box. These teams of four will race to be the first to roll their box over the finish line. This has high injury potential, so use caution. You could also have the students just roll the boxes without anyone inside them.

• **Self-Propelled Roll-a-Box.** Use the same set-up as "Roll-a-Box," but two people squat on their hands and knees inside each box. To race, they crawl forward to make the box roll (imagine two hamsters in a wheel). First to reach the finish line wins.

• **Boxy Free-for-Alls.** If you like chaos, try these two variations. For each one you want four people to stand together inside a box, like in the "Vertical Blind Relay." Set up some boundaries for the playing area, and assign one person to stand near each box to help give directions. Now choose one box to be "It," and play tag.

Or let the boxed players roam around the playing area, and give Frisbees to every player who's not inside a box so those players can play "dodge box." Give points to students for every box they hit, and award a prize to the box that's hit the fewest times during the game. *Jim Walton*

PIZZA-BOX FLIP

When the pizza party comes to an end and your kids are just milling around and waiting for their rides home, start a little contest. Tape the empty pizza boxes shut and set up a couple of target tables 20 feet away from the throw line. Contestants will toss the pizza boxes like Frisbees and try to hit the table. Award extra points if the box lands on the table without hanging over the edges. And double a student's points if he makes sure the pizza boxes end up in the trashcan before he leaves! *Ken Lane*

PLANET BALL

In movies and on television shows, aliens are usually portrayed as brilliant creatures with great power and control. However, in this game the aliens (your youth group members) will have to prove how bright they are during an out-of-this-world version of basketball.

You'll need three kickballs or playground balls that are three different colors and sizes to represent Jupiter, Saturn, and Mars. You'll also need a playing area that has one basketball hoop and a three-point line. The area inside the basketball three-point line (the semi-circle) is called the solar system, and that's where all the scoring takes place. The area outside the three-point line is called outer space—that's where the aliens wait for their turn to play (see diagram).

Two teams of at least six aliens play against each other. The object of the game is to get any of the balls into the hoop. A Jupiter is worth three points, and it's scored when the largest ball makes a basket. A basket made with Saturn, or the medium-size ball, is worth two points. The Mars ball, or the smallest ball, is worth one point. Each team gets five minutes to try to score points, and then they switch with the other team to play defense while the other team plays offense for five minutes.

Only three offensive aliens are allowed inside the solar system at a time, each with a planet ball in hand. And they aren't coordinated enough to dribble the ball, so they just run around with it. The three offensive aliens must remain in the solar system until they've taken a shot by bouncing, kneeing, or heading the ball into the hoop. After taking a shot, whether points were scored or not, the shooter retrieves the ball, leaves the solar system, and gives the planet ball to one of the teammates lined up in outer space, waiting for their turn to enter the solar system.

There are also only three defense-playing aliens inside the shooting area at a time. Their teammates are standing in another line in outer space, waiting and watching for their turn in the solar system. The three defensive aliens try to block shots or get in the way of the offensive players. However, they are only allowed the same amount of body contact as in a regular game of basketball. If anyone plays too roughly, that person's team receives a one-point deduction. In addition, if a defensive player picks up a planet ball, another point is lost.

Whenever a basket is scored, all the defensive players must tag alien teammates in outer space to replace them. The tagged players then hurry in and help with defense. That means that as soon as any points are scored, the offensive team has an opportunity to try to quickly score again while the defensive team is substituting players.

Any planet ball that lands in outer space must be given back to the offensive player who was trying to make a basket. If that player hasn't taken a shot yet, she'll have to

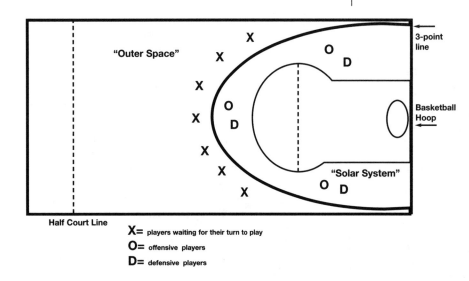

"Outer Space"

3-point line

Basketball Hoop

"Solar System"

Half Court Line

X= players waiting for their turn to play
O= offensive players
D= defensive players

wait in the solar system for the ball. Aliens are less coordinated in outer space, so when they're outside the solar system, they can only move the ball by carrying or hitting it with their elbows.

If there is a tie at the end of the initial 10 minutes of play, the teams play again; but this time they each play offensively for only two minutes. *Chard Berndt*

BIBLE BASKETBALL

You can either use this game to review a Bible lesson or just to test your kids' Bible-trivia knowledge. You'll need a list of Bible-trivia questions (see the sample list below), a basketball hoop, and a basketball. (A child-size basketball hoop and ball work well for this game.) Mark off an area around the goal where the teenagers should stand to shoot the ball.

Create two teams and pick one person from each to do the "jump ball." In the "jump ball," you ask a trivia question and the first person to get it right gets two points and a chance to shoot the basketball for an additional two points. That person's team also gets to go first.

Now give the team who won the jump ball a trivia question. Team members can discuss the question before giving their answer, but no Bibles, lesson books, or other resources may be consulted. If they get the right answer, then they get two points and a chance to shoot the ball for another two. After they've taken their shot, it's the other team's turn to receive a question.

If the first team does not get the right answer, their opponent has a chance to steal. This is called a free throw. Free throws are worth one point and a chance to shoot the ball for another point, if they make the first shot.

Fouls may be called on a team that displays poor sportsmanship, cheats, or exhibits a lack of teamwork. If a foul occurs, the other team gets to shoot a free throw.

Everyone on a team should be given a chance to shoot the ball. The first team to reach a predetermined number of points (or whichever team has the most points when you run out of questions) is the winner.

The following 30 sample questions (and the correct answers in parentheses) will get you started. *Stacy Goebel*

1. How many books are in the Old Testament? (39)
2. How many disciples were there? (12)
3. Who was swallowed by a whale? (Jonah)
4. Moses had a brother and a sister. What were their names? (Aaron and Miriam)
5. Who was turned into a pillar of salt? (Lot's wife)
6. Which Bible character's name means "encourager"? (Barnabas)
7. What does B.C. mean? (before Christ)
8. Name the four Gospel books in the New Testament (Matthew, Mark, Luke, and John)
9. Who wrote the book of Genesis? (Moses)
10. How many books are in the New Testament? (27)
11. Saul became Paul on the road to where? (Damascus)
12. Who was David's best friend? (Jonathan)
13. Isaac had twin sons, and one stole the birthright from the other. What were their names? (Jacob and Esau)
14. Which disciple was a tax collector before he met Jesus? (Matthew)
15. Who betrayed Jesus? (Judas Iscariot)
16. Who lost everything—family, money, property—and still remained faithful to God? (Job)
17. Which king in the Bible is known for his great wisdom? (Solomon)
18. What was the name of the man who found no guilt in Jesus, but sentenced him anyway due to pressure from the people? (Pontius Pilate)
19. How many plagues were cast on Egypt before Pharaoh let Moses and the Israelites go? (10)
20. Whose strength was in his hair? (Samson)
21. How many books are there in the Bible? (66)
22. Who was so short that he climbed up in a tree to see Jesus, and what kind of tree did he climb? (Zacchaeus and a sycamore tree)
23. What was the name of the giant David killed? (Goliath)
24. When Noah built the ark, how long did the rain last? (40 days and 40 nights)
25. Who baptized Jesus? (John the Baptist)
26. Who led the tribes of Israel after Moses died? (Joshua)
27. What was the name of the king who ordered that the baby Jesus be killed? (Herod)
28. What is the last book of the Bible? (Revelation)

29. Who denied Jesus three times? (Peter)
30. Name four fruits of the Spirit. (love, joy, peace, patience, kindness, goodness, gentleness, faithfulness, and self-control)

ARCTIC BOWLING

Create some frozen bowling balls by filling gallon plastic milk jugs with different amounts of water and place them on their sides in a freezer so the handles are sticking up. This will give you bowling balls of different weights—just like in a real bowling alley. Make a lot of them because the students will go through them in a hurry.

Set up your alley by placing sheets of plastic on the floor. Then turn a table on its side at the end of each "lane" to serve as a backstop. About a foot in front of each table, set up 10 two-liter soda bottles half full of water in a typical 10-pin formation.

Divide your group into teams of four to six students, assign each team a lane, and give them a couple of frozen bowling balls to use. Remind them to slide or roll the milk jugs, rather than toss them. (Throwing them makes the ice inside break up faster and shortens the life of the ball.)

To keep the games moving, create a rotation so that after each teenager bowls, he moves down to the end of his lane and takes a turn resetting the pins. Award cups of crushed ice to the highest scoring team or individual after everyone has bowled 10 frames. *Glenn Lyle*

BOMBARDMENT

You need an indestructible room, 12 plastic bowling pins or two-liter soda bottles, and four to six volleyballs. Mark a line down the middle of your playing area. Create teams of six players, but only two teams will play at a time. Have each team stand on its half of the court, and give each player a bowling pin. Ask the kids to write their names on pieces of masking tape and stick them to their pins for identification purposes. Players should spread out the pins along their team's wall, setting the pins about two feet in front of it. Once the game begins, players are not allowed to touch their pins.

To start, give each team half the volleyballs. The object of the game is to use the volleyballs to

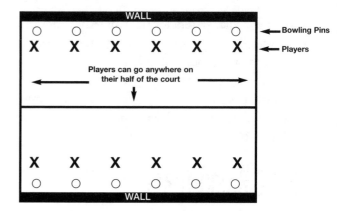

knock over the other team's bowling pins from behind the centerline. Players can stop the throws of their opponents by catching, kicking, smacking, or even head-butting the ball—anything goes (within reason, of course). If a player's pin is knocked over, that person is out of the game. Have leaders standing near the walls so they can pull players from the game when their pins are toppled.

The last team to have a pin still standing is the winner. Set a time limit for each game, which will allow you to create a tournament between several teams so more students can participate. *Jeff Hicks*

TABLETOP BOWLING

Groups from two to 200 can have lots of fun when you create a mini-bowling alley in your youth group room. And the best part—no one has to wear those ugly rental shoes! To make the lanes, just push two or three six- to eight-foot-long tables together lengthwise. Set up 10 pins in the standard bowling-pin formation at the far end of each lane. You can use real bowling pins, plastic two-liter soda bottles that are half full of water, tin cans, paper cups—you get the idea. For bowling balls, use balls of any size

BOWL-O-RAMA

NAME	1	2	3	4	5	6	7	8	9	10	TOTAL
1.											
2.											
3.											
4.											

(basketballs, volleyballs, soccer balls, softballs) or be completely different and use Frisbees! To add some realism to the game, try to get some score cards from your local bowling alley or create your own (see sample).

Form bowling teams of four to six students, and let each team choose a lane. Set up a rotation so that the last person to bowl moves to the end of the lane to reset the pins. After 10 frames, award some cheap plastic bowling trophies to the highest bowler or team. *Derek Ellison*

DIZZY KNOCK-DOWN

Create the atmosphere of a county fair or carnival in your youth room with just one game booth. Set up some tables around the perimeter of the room and create a pyramid of large plastic or Styrofoam cups on each one.

Students form teams of at least four players. Each team should stand about 10 feet away from one of the stations. As each player's turn comes, she is blindfolded and takes five throws of a tennis ball or softball to knock down the cups. Another player verbally guides the blindfolded thrower, while the two other teammates retrieve the thrown balls and toss them back to the guide.

Before each throw, the blindfolded player should turn in about five or 10 circles so she gets nice and dizzy. After each toss of the ball, the guide tells his teammate how to correct the next throw—higher or lower, more to the right or to the left, and so on.

After five tosses, the players should rotate to new positions on their teams and let someone else try to knock down the cups. *Ken Lane*

HOMEMADE CLAY RECIPE

Ingredients:
1 cup all-purpose flour
½ cup salt
2 tsp. cream of tartar
1 cup water
1 tbsp. vegetable oil
Food coloring

In a saucepan, mix flour, salt, and cream of tartar over medium heat. Stir in water, oil, and food coloring. When adding the food coloring, start by adding a few drops at a time and stirring it in to see the color. You can always add more of the same color or experiment by mixing colors. It's a good idea to make at least two shades of green, one light and one dark. Some color examples are powder blue (15 drops red, 15 drops blue), turquoise (5 drops green, 15 drops blue), lime green (two drops green, 18 drops yellow), and violet (15 drops red, five drops blue).

Cook over medium heat, stirring constantly with a spatula until a ball forms (three to five minutes). When the dough becomes rubbery and pulls away from the sides of the saucepan, it's finished cooking. Knead the warm ball of fresh dough and store it in an airtight container at room temperature to keep it from drying out. It should last for months. *Laurie Howard*

PLAY-DOH MINI-GOLF

Not only is this a fun way to entertain lots of kids and adults, but everyone can help design the course. You can make it any size you like and play inside or outside. For each hole of golf you plan to play, you'll need a sheet of plywood or poster board for the hole and fairway. You'll also need tables, a batch of clay or Play-Doh—a different color for each hole (see **Homemade Clay Recipe**)—and a shoebox full of items to design the hole. Use popsicle sticks or toothpicks for tree trunks, bridges, and flagpoles; blue construction paper for water traps; sand or brown sugar for sand traps; and implements like glue and scissors to help each team create a masterpiece. Be creative! Throw in other miscellaneous items like bottle caps, pipe cleaners, buttons, and the like, and see what teams come up with on their own. You can also make signs for a pro shop, a clubhouse, the name of the golf course, and a welcome to tournament visitors.

For the last hole, you can paint a clown's face on a quarter-inch piece of plywood, cut a hole in the mouth, and set up a ramp to the opening.

Make some homemade golfing trophies by gluing ping-pong balls on top of cans and spray-painting them gold. Or plan to give out other silly prizes like golf tees and golf balls.

To set up each hole and fairway, place a sheet of plywood or poster board, a ball of play dough, and a box of craft goodies on each table. Establish your design teams of six to eight players, and assign each team a hole to design and create. Give teams about 20 minutes to complete their work. Once all the holes are finished, number them and begin play. Have each team begin with their hole and then work their way around the entire course.

Use corn-pop cereal for golf balls and pretzel sticks for golf clubs. Or give the players real miniature golf putters and balls and let them try their luck at sinking balls. Provide index cards and golf pencils so teams can keep track of their scores.

When every team has finished the course, award prizes to individuals or teams for the lowest score, wildest technique, best putt, best use of materials to create a hole, and so on. *Laurie Howard*

Glow-in-the-Dark Broom Hockey

This game takes quite a bit of prep work, but it's well worth the effort, and it's a blast to play! You need a broom and a plain white T-shirt for each player. Either ask your kids to bring in some old T-shirts or buy cheap packs of men's undershirts to use. You also need two colors of glow-in-the-dark paint, a roll of glow-in-the-dark tape, a playground ball that glows in the dark (you could paint a regular ball if necessary), and two cardboard boxes for goals.

A day or two before playing this game, take half the T-shirts and paint a large X with one color of paint on the front and back of each one. Then paint an O with the other color on each side of the remaining T-shirts. You can also provide glow-in-the-dark headbands in the same colors for the participants to wear. Paint the two cardboard boxes with the glow-in-the-dark paint, again one of each color.

Set up the playing field by taping boundary lines on the floor with the glow-in-the-dark tape and placing the goal boxes at either end of the field. Put coverings over the windows to insure complete darkness when the lights are off.

Now choose teams of six players. Have the players don their T-shirts, grab their brooms, and get into position on the field. Place the ball in the center of the field, turn off the lights, and let 'em go for it like in a real game of hockey! Turn on the lights at irregular intervals to check on players, to make substitutions, or whenever a goal is scored. The highest scoring team wins. *Kurt Reeder*

Spoon Hockey

Empty out your silverware drawer before playing this one! You need 10 to 14 dinner spoons, four large serving spoons, a tennis ball, and four orange cones. Use two cones at each end of the playing area to set up a four-foot-wide goal. You need two teams of five to seven players. Each team should choose a goalie who will use two large serving spoons to defend her goal. The rest of the players get a dinner spoon for hitting the tennis ball up and down the field. It's not a very fast-paced game because the teams must play on their knees. For comfort and safety, you may want to hand out kneepads and safety goggles.

To start, place the tennis ball in the middle of the field for the opening face-off, then play the game with regular hockey rules. If you're playing with a larger group, you can rotate new players into the game every four minutes or have more people play on each team, but then use two tennis balls. *Steve Dallwig*

Toilet-Brush Hockey

Use toilet brushes for hockey sticks, a small soccer net or two folding chairs for each goal area, and a mesh sponge (or something that will slide easily but won't cause injury when it's airborne) for a puck. Each goalie gets a plastic dustpan and rubber gloves to use to defend her goal.

It's best if you form teams of five kids or so, with one goalie and four offensive players on each team. To involve more students, you can also play two games simultaneously, side by side in a gym or another large room.

Play 10-minute games, using traditional hockey rules with face-offs, fouls, player substitutions, penalty boxes, and so forth. If you have time, you can set up a round-robin tournament. Depending on the number of teams you have, you can usually play an entire tournament in about two or three hours. At the end of the tourney, the winning team should be awarded Lord Stanley's Toilet Brush, which is just a toilet brush that has been spray-painted silver and mounted on a piece of wood. *Paul Snyder*

CD Game Timer

When your youth group is playing a highly competitive and absorbing game like soccer or broom hockey, it can be tedious to keep track of the time for player or team rotations. Sometimes the person who's supposed be watching the clock gets so wrapped up in the game that he forgets to do his job.

Next time try using music as your timing mechanism. Bring out the boom box and load it up with several fun and fast-paced CDs. Play the CDs randomly and have players rotate in or out every time the song changes. The kids can hear the song coming to an end, so the players on the floor can get ready to come out while the players on the sidelines prepare to take their turn. A bonus benefit: It really helps cut down on complaints that one group is getting to play longer than another one. *David Smitley*

Plunger Soccer

Provide a plunger for each player (you can probably find some cheap ones at a dollar store). Establish the boundaries of your playing area, including a centerline and a goal at each end.

Divide the group into two even teams and send teams to opposite ends of the room. Each team should choose a goalie to stand in front of their goal area. The rest of the players stand in four or five horizontal lines between the centerline and their goal.

The object of the game is to knock the ball (playground ball, softball, soccer ball, whatever you choose to use) into the opposing team's goal, using only their plungers—no hands, feet, heads, or other body parts may touch the ball. Players are allowed to move left or right, but not forward or backward on the playing field. Imagine the motion that takes place on a foosball table, and you've got the right idea. The first team to score 15 points wins! *Gordon Dickinson*

Toilet Paper Roll

Tape off a rectangular area about three feet by six feet, and set up your starting line 15 to 20 feet away.

Line up your players along the starting line. Give each person a roll of toilet paper and a plunger. (Players could put their initials on their rolls of toilet paper for easier identification and scoring.)

At the blow of a whistle or the bellow of a youth leader, players use their plungers to push the rolls of toilet paper—as in a game of shuffleboard—toward the scoring box at the other end of the room. Give three points for every roll that lands inside the lines of tape and one point for any that ends up within a plunger's distance of the rectangle.

Depending on the size of your group, students could be allowed to take more than one turn and accumulate more points for the win. Or you could turn it into a tournament style of play and eliminate players who can't get their roll close enough to the box. Eventually you'll end up with a champion plunger! *Ken Lane*

Plunger Push

This game is very similar to Toilet Paper Roll, but you need a trashcan to score points instead of a rectangle of tape. Another difference is that players balance the roll of toilet paper on the rubber part of their plunger before making the TP airborne in the direction of the trashcan from 15 feet away. The player who makes the most baskets wins. *Ken Lane*

Two-Table Ping-Pong

Set up two ping-pong tables end to end with about three feet between them, and you'll end up with a table over 20 feet long. Remove the nets, and the three-foot gap now acts as your net.

Two to four players play a normal game of ping-pong, except the ball can bounce as many times as necessary, just as long as it jumps from table to table. For longer volleys, add some cardboard walls on both sides of the table, including on the sides of the gap. *Bobby Moss*

Ace the Spades

Have you ever been waiting for the bulk of your students to arrive and needed a great, short, athletic game? If so, next time try this fun volleyball skills game with a twist. All you need are three players, a volleyball, and an open wall (meaning there's nothing valuable sitting in front of it, such as the youth leader). A net is optional. Set up the playing field according to the diagram below.

The server stands behind the back line to serve the volleyball. The other two players, called spades, stand on the other side of the court between the front service line and the wall (call this area the target zone). When the ball is served into the target zone, the two spades must cooperate (even though they're really opponents) as they try to hit the ball no more than three times to make it land behind the back service line. Whenever the spades do this successfully, they each score one point.

On the other hand, if the server aces the spades by serving the ball into the target zone so they can't return it over the back line using only three hits, then the server receives a point. Each round is played to five points.

At the conclusion of each round, every player moves one spot counter clockwise—the server becomes a spade, that spade moves to become the second spade, who moves off the court to join the

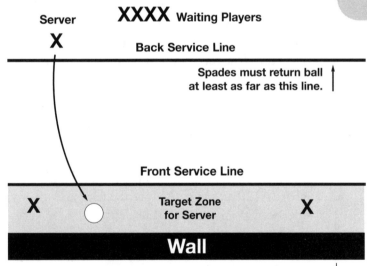

Server
XXXX Waiting Players
X
Back Service Line
Spades must return ball
at least as far as this line. ↑
Front Service Line
X   Target Zone   X
for Server
Wall

line of waiting players, and a new server moves in. The winner is the person who has the most points after all the rounds. *Kevin Turner*

WHEELCHAIR RACE

Gather as many wheelchairs as you can. Plan to have a person in each wheelchair and a person pushing it. Before the kids show up, construct a course out of folding tables, cardboard boxes, and

PANTYHOSE PADDLE

Here's a piece of game equipment you can easily make for people of all athletic abilities to use while playing a variety of games. All you need are wire coat hangers and old nylons large enough to stretch over the hangers.

Reshape each hanger into a circle, keeping the hook part intact so it can be used as a handle. Carefully stretch a piece of nylon over each hanger. You now you have a great racket for hitting lightweight balls.

Use it for a game of volleyball, where players hit a Nerf or wiffle ball over the net, using the paddle instead of their arms and hands. Or try using it as a bat in a game of lightweight baseball.

There's also nylon lacrosse, where two players whip the ball back and forth at one another using these great rackets. Or how about nylon basketball? Players simply dribble a small rubber ball down the court using their paddles. The possibilities are endless. Just use your imagination! *Brian Morgan*

so on. For extra fun, go out the back door and put out an orange cone they must go around. When the kids show up, don't let them in just yet. Pair them off, give each pair a wheelchair (you can do this in shifts if you don't have enough chairs for your pairs), and blindfold the driver. The passenger must give verbal directions to the driver to get through the course. Each pair must go through the course, out the door, around the cone, and back through the course to the starting point. The fastest pair wins—or don't have anybody win, just have the fun of laughing yourselves silly. It's good to remind them of Matthew 5:3 after this exercise— inheriting the Kingdom of Heaven comes through reliance upon God. *Dan Perryman*

BODY SNATCHERS

Put your group in a dark building at night. Choose two to be body snatchers. The object of the game is to survive.

Turn the players loose first, then the two body

snatchers. Players can hide or run, whatever they think is safest. When a body snatcher tags a player, that player becomes a body snatcher and joins in the hunt. A minute ago, your best friend was by your side, but he's been out of sight for a few minutes...Players soon discover that after the first few minutes of the game, they can't trust anybody. The last human being left wins the game and has the option of being a body snatcher for the next round.

Brian Stegner

AIR SHOW

You'll need two sheets of paper per player, plus scissors, pens, markers, crayons, tape, and so on. If you can play this game around a balcony, that's even better.

Students make two paper airplanes each and compete in four contests: a distance contest, a design contest, an acrobatic contest, and a target contest. Have the kids and leaders all vote on the design and acrobatic contests. For the target contest, designate a circle on the ground or against a wall that kids must aim for. Designate a winner (or a first-, second-, and third-place winner) in each of the four contests and for overall performance.

• **Air Raid.** Designate a country with various cities and towns—more than one country if you want. Think about territories ahead of time—you need a territory for each team, plus one neutral territory. Have players start off with two fresh paper planes they've made, and divide them into two teams. Their airplanes are now an air force—have them give their air force a name based on a theme (for example, with a breakfast cereal theme they might come up with the Captain Crunches or the Lucky Charms). They should quickly design a simple insignia to differentiate their planes from the other air force's planes.

Assign each team its territory, and explain the neutral territory. Each team must stand behind a line in their territory to throw planes. Planes that land within their own territory cost two points. Planes that land in neutral territory gain three points, and planes that land in enemy territory gain five points. If a plane lands outside all the targets, no points are given or taken away. Once a plane is thrown, no one may touch it.

Start the kids off and watch the planes fly! When the war is over, carefully note each plane's location and insignia and count up the points. It's a good tip to have everybody leave the scene of battle without touching anything after the war ends.

Brian Stegner

VOLUNTEER HULA HOOP TOSS

Your props for this game are several hula hoops and one brave, noble, self-sacrificing adult volunteer.

Line the players up across your available area. Have the volunteer sit on the floor with her legs crossed and her back to the players, 10 to 15 feet away from them.

Players take turns tossing hula hoops toward the volunteer, trying to ring her with a hoop. To add to the challenge, have each player close his eyes, then spin him around five times before he throws. You can point him in the right direction after spinning him, but if you've done your job, it won't help much.

After players have witnessed the survival of the volunteer, they can take turns volunteering. This can be encouraged if the first volunteer acts like she has the most fun, most dangerous job in the world. *Ken Lane*

ZORKS

Find the *only* Golden Key that unlocks the space station (church) door from the inside, and escape from this station—which is set to self-destruct in T-minus-three hours. Your leaders (preferably dressed in black) are the Zorks, who sneak around and capture the players so they can't find the Golden Key. Play the game inside the church with 10 to 30 players—leaders (Zorks) versus kids.

Allow plenty of time to prepare. You'll need the following supplies.
- The Golden Key (any key)
- The Liberating Light (flashlight)
- Freedom Flags (white handkerchiefs or pieces of cloth) Have more flags than you have kids playing the game.
- Clues written on slips of paper
- Large balloons

Decide where you'll hide the following items. Hide them after you finish the preparations.

- Golden Key (Conceal it well. Make the kids find and use the clues to get the key. Don't leave it in.a place where they might stumble onto it accidentally because then the game will be over.)
- Liberating Light
- Freedom Flags
- Balloons with clues to the Liberating Light

Decide which leaders will be the Zorkian King, who gives clues to the Freedom Flags, and the Zorkian Lair Commander, who guards the captured players. Make these final preparations.

- Designate a place in the church to be the Zorks' lair—maybe the fellowship hall.
- Write as many clues as you want to the location of the Liberating Light. Insert the clues into balloons, which you'll need to blow up and hide around the church. Save one clue to begin the game.
- Write down the *only* clue to the Golden Key's location, and tape it to the Liberating Light.
- Hide the Freedom Flags throughout the church.
- Write clues to Freedom Flag locations on slips of paper. Don't insert these clues into balloons—the Zorkian King hands out these clues when players find him.

To begin the game, gather the students in a central location. Explain their mission and give them one starting clue to help them find the Liberating Light.

- They must escape this space station before it self-destructs.
- To escape they must find the Golden Key, which will unlock the door to the outside.
- The only clue for the Golden Key is taped to the Liberating Light.
- Clues to the Liberating Light are hidden inside balloons throughout the church. When they find balloons, they'll have more clues to the location of the Liberating Light.
- Warn them that Zorks sneak around, capture players, and take them into their lair.
- To free captured players teammates must find the Zorkian King, get one of his clues, use it

to locate a Freedom Flag, and trade the Freedom Flag for the teammate's release.

- No one can enter the lair to rescue a captive without a Freedom Flag.
- The Zorkian King does not attack or take victims to the lair—he only gives out clues to Freedom Flag locations when the students find him.
- They're more likely to escape before destruction if they work as a team with everyone looking for clues.

Turn off all the lights, and close all the doors. Then turn them loose in the church. Beware the Zorks!

SQUEEZE AND GRAB

Break your group into two teams and form two parallel lines of players sitting down and holding hands. Everyone in the line must look toward the back of the line or keep their eyes closed—except the first person in the line. No talking during this game. Place an object on the floor between the last person in one line and the last person in the other line. To start, flip a coin. If it's heads, the person in the front of each line begins the squeeze. The squeeze continues from person to person. When the players at the end of each line feel their hands squeezed, they grab for an item placed between them. The winning team rotates one position forward. If the coin lands tails, neither team is supposed to squeeze. If one or both teams have a false squeeze, they rotate backward one position. For more fun, use a banana as the item passed; at the end of the game, one person eats the banana.

WHAT'S MY NAME?

This game is fun for groups that don't know each other well. As kids arrive, write their names in large letters on squares of paper. When all the students have arrived, safety pin the papers on their backs, give them cards and pencils and tell them to write the names of as many people as possible while trying not to let anyone write theirs. The only rule is that kids can't stand with their backs against the wall. The winner is the person whose name appears on people's cards the fewest number of times.

BLIND LINE

Start by brainstorming a list of memorable lines—popular slogans, phrases, movie lines, lyrics, Scripture—from the audience. You may want to give some samples to get the group going—
• Did you brush your teeth?
• Merry Christmas!
• Mary had a little lamb.
• Make my day!

Write each line on a separate piece of paper and distribute two lines to each player (as many players as it takes for you to get rid of all your slips of paper). Give your players a scene to act out (for example, you arrive at school and a new statue of a ballerina is on the front lawn). They must deliver their lines as soon as they can during the scene. The scene ends when all lines have been delivered or when you call time.

FREEZE TAG DRAMA

Two players face the audience, and two others have their backs to the audience. The two players facing the audience start the scene based on a suggestion from the audience—something involving lots of action. At some point the third player yells, "Freeze" and switches places with one of the two actors, assuming the same exact position on stage. The replaced actor takes the position of the new actor with his back to the audience. The new player begins a new scene based on the position he has assumed. The scene continues until the fourth player yells, "Freeze" and takes one of the places to begin a new scene. Keep rotating players as long as it remains entertaining.

LIVING ROOM
GAMES

No access to a fellowship hall or gymnasium? Then try some of these games, all of which can be played in a living room. They're great for informal gatherings, parties, or anytime you've got a roomful of people just sitting around. Some are quiet games that involve little action, others require some moving around. No need to limit yourself to living rooms, of course, for you can play many of these games practically anywhere—on road trips, during those long arena waits before a concert begins, etc.

BIBLE BALDERDASH

The regular rules of Balderdash apply in this game, but instead of using a dictionary, collect obscure and outrageous words and place names from the Bible.

Divide the students into teams of six to eight players. Read and spell each word for the entire group, then give team members some time to work together to come up with a phony definition for the word, write it down, and hand it in to you. Read all the definitions aloud to the group, including the real one.

Now teams try to guess which definition is the real one and then cast their vote by a show of hands as you read each definition again. Give a group one point for choosing the correct definition, and two points whenever another team votes for their made-up definition. This should encourage students to make their definitions sound somewhat believable.

Malcolm McMillan

Praetorium - originally a Greek word referring to a place where Roman leaders would meet. (Matthew 27:27)

Ehud - A left-handed man in the Old Testament who killed a very fat king by stabbing him through with a double-edged sword, which was swallowed up by the king's belly. (Judges 3:15-30)

Nimrim - A place near the Dead Sea in Moab, noted for its great watering holes. (Isaiah 15:6; Jeremiah 48:34)

Sanballat - An influential Samaritan who tried to stop the Israelites from rebuilding the walls of Jerusalem. (Nehemiah 4:1)

EMOTION MOTION

How you say something can be just as important as the words you use. Before playing this game, create some "Say It Like You Mean It" cards, one per student. On each card write six statements like the examples on page 62. You can either give all the players the same card, give a different card to each group of players, or give a different card to each student. It all depends on how much time you have to spend preparing for this game. You'll also need a copy of the **Emotion Motion Game Board** (page 65), a die for each group, and a game piece for each player (M&Ms or other hard-shell candies work well).

Divide students into groups of four to eight. Designate a space on the game board to be the starting point where players set their game pieces. Players take turns rolling the die and moving their pieces accordingly. Once a player has landed on a new space, she looks at her Say It Like You Mean It card and finds the statement that matches the number on the die. Before her turn ends, she must say the phrase out loud, in a tone that conveys the emotion that's written on the space where her game piece is sitting.

For example, assume players were using the Say

Say It Like You Mean It

Read the statement next to the number that matches the number you just rolled with the die.

1. I have to go to the bathroom.
2. Count from one to ten.
3. Just take a moment and think.
4. I like chicken.
5. Do you want to go to lunch?
6. I don't know.

It Like You Mean It sample card above. Say a player rolls a six and then moves his game piece six spaces to land on the "Sad" space. Now he must say, "I don't know" (phrase number six) in a sad tone of voice.

As a twist, the rest of the group can vote to send the current player back two spaces if his tone isn't convincing. Using the earlier example, someone could choose to challenge player number one, saying he didn't sound sad enough. Then the rest of the group would vote. If they vote unanimously that player one didn't sound sad, then he has to move his game piece back two spaces. However, if the vote isn't unanimous, he can leave his game piece where he initially landed.

The first person to reach the last space on the board is the winner. If you're using some type of candy for game pieces, let the winner eat the rest of the bag as a prize. *Susan Grapengater*

PLAY-DOH PICTIONARY

All you need for this home version of the commercial game Pictionary is a lump of clay for every team and ideas for things the players will make with it. A homemade clay recipe is on page 53.

Give each team of six to eight students a generous lump of clay. At the beginning of each round, the first sculptors should come to you or another leader so they can be quietly told the item they're going to attempt to create with the clay.

Here are some sculptable items you can use for a game: peas in a pod, corn on the cob, a hot dog, a cowboy hat, a Porsche, a diamond, a gorilla, the Empire State Building, one of the youth group leaders, a toilet, the school mascot, current music, movie, or television stars. As you can see, nearly anything can be formed with Play-Doh! And if your group is more into abstracts, give them a chance to try some of these challenging sculptures: a riddle wrapped inside an enigma, relativism, the Environmental Protection Agency, the NBA Players Association, confusion, or sterility.

When the players return to their teams, they must wait for the signal to begin the sculpting race. And as soon as they've begun to mold the Play-Doh, their teammates can try to guess what the object is. The first team to answer correctly wins a point for

Emotion Motion

that round.

Play enough rounds so every kid has a chance to be a sculptor. Total up the points and declare a winner. Give the winning team all the containers of Play-Doh and ask them to create their own Play-Doh Pictionary trophy. *Marshall Allen*

MELLOW COPS AND ROBBERS

All you need is a deck of cards and 20 players. Ahead of time determine which cards will be the cop and robber cards. For example, you could choose the king of spades to be the cop and the jack of diamonds to be the robber. To make sure someone draws the cop and robber cards, use only as many cards as you have players and be sure to include your cop and robber cards in the stack.

This is a silent game where the robber tries to eliminate people by covertly winking at them. At the same time, the cop is trying to catch the robber before she can eliminate everyone in the circle. When someone sees the robber wink at him, he should silently count to 10 and then say, "I've been robbed," while backing out of the circle a few paces. Ousted players can continue to watch the game in silence. Players who are not the cop or robber should be careful not to give away the robber's identity.

The cop is allowed three guesses per round as to who the robber is. He can make his guesses at any time. If the robber should wink at the cop, then the cop shows her his card and says, "You're busted!" Other than robbed players and the cop, there should be no talking during each round.

Have the group sit in a large circle where everyone can face each other. Identify the cop and robber cards for the players, then deal the cards. Players can look at their cards, but they shouldn't show them to anyone. Now the game begins and the winks and accusations fly! When only five people remain, including the cop and the robber, declare the robber the winner of that round. And obviously, if the cop correctly guesses the identity of the robber, then he's the winner.

Bring everyone back into the circle, collect and shuffle the cards, and redistribute them for the next round. You can vary each round by adding more robbers or cops into the fray. This is a great, quiet game of observation and strategy. *Jeff Daniels and Walter Parker Jr.*

HOMICIDE 101

Give each group of three to five players a copy of **Homicide Report** (page 67) and 15 minutes to read the handout and work together to come up with an answer. When the time is up, have a member from each group read their homicide report to the rest of the youth group. *Len Cuthbert*

CLEARING CUSTOMS

This is a variation of the kids' travel game where you fill an imaginary suitcase with items that begin with each letter of the alphabet. In this version the youth sit in a circle and the first player says, as though they're speaking to a customs agent, "I've been on vacation, and I'm only bringing back a _____." And they finish the statement by naming any item they choose.

The next person in the circle now says the same phrase but adds the name of an item that begins with the *last* letter of the previous item. Then the third person repeats the phrase, but they must say the previous two items as *one word* and then add their item, which begins with the last letter of the second person's item.

Here's an example:
Youth 1: "I've been on vacation, and I'm only bringing back a cat."
Youth 2: "I've been on vacation, and I'm only bringing back a cat and a tap."
Youth 3: "I've been on vacation, and I'm only bringing back a catap and a pig."
Youth 4: "I've been on vacation, and I'm only bringing back a catapig and a gift."
Youth 5: "I've been on vacation, and I'm only bringing back a catapigift and a torch."
Youth 6: "I've been on vacation, and I'm only bringing back a catapigiftorch and a hat."

Got it? Rather than eliminate people, award points to those who are successful. To keep it simple for the first couple times through, limit the words to one syllable. As players catch on, make the game more challenging by allowing longer words. You can also vary the game by limiting the words to certain categories like animals, foods, and so on. *Len Cuthbert*

Homicide Report

Solve the following crime scene by writing your own original and creative story involving the following pieces of evidence.

1. Mrs. Greenhorn is dead, lying at the bottom of the stairs that lead to the second floor of her home. She has a massive head wound but no other injuries (broken bones, etc.).

2. She has a banana in one hand and a hair dryer in the other.

3. The door of the refrigerator in the kitchen has been left open.

4. A frying pan is on the floor at the top of the stairs.

5. The window in the second floor bathroom is broken and open.

Phone Book Phables

Give each small group of players a phone book (with a white pages section), a piece of paper, and something to write with. Now ask each team to take about 10 minutes to create a story at least 10 words long using only last names from the white pages section of the phone book. Words may be used phonetically—in other words, they don't have to be spelled correctly.

Here's an example sentence using last names: Abbott Ait Tollett Tisue, Wile Ritchey Swisher Begien Reeping Wildman Oates. Read it like this: "Abbot ate toilet tissue, while Ritchey Swisher began reaping wild-man oats."

Ask a representative from each group to read that group's story out loud, then take a vote to see which one the youth group liked best. *Tom Bartlett*

Phone Book Scavenger Hunt

Order some extra Yellow Pages phone books from your local phone company, or use recycled phone books at the end of the year. Choose 12 phone numbers for different businesses and write some clues, one for each number. For example, you might write, "I have a skunk in my house and I want it removed without killing it. Please find me the number for Ace Animal Control."

To play, divide the students into as many groups as you have phone books. Read the first clue out loud a couple of times to make sure everyone heard it. The first group to find the correct phone number should send a member of their team to the front of the room to confirm their answer with you. If correct, that team gets 100 points. If not, the representative returns to the team and they try again. Give the second and third teams to answer correctly 50 and 25 points, respectively.

This will be trickier to play than you might think. Many items aren't listed under the category you'd expect. When you've read all the clues, tally the points and give fabulous prizes to the winning team—their very own copies of last year's Yellow Pages directory. *Susan Grapengater*

Chewy Gooey Clues

Play this game with your junior highers to get rid of leftover holiday candy. You need at least 10 different kinds of mini-candy bars or other candy. To prepare for the game, unwrap each piece of candy and sort the candy into Styrofoam cups. Write the name of each candy on the bottom of the cup and tape or staple each empty wrapper onto a 3x5 card.

Now form two teams and choose one person from each to go first. The players must close their eyes and taste the candy in the first cup. Put a minute on the timer as both players try to describe to their team what it tastes like, feels like, smells like, and so on. The teams shout out their guesses until one of them guesses the correct identity of the candy or until a minute is up on the clock. Give the winning team five points for every correct guess and show the candy wrapper to affirm the right answer. Now two new players take a turn with the next kind of candy. The game continues until all the candy is gone. Total the points for both teams, and announce the winner. *Keith Curran*

Coin-Bounce Bathroom Dash

Two teams of six players sit around a table, with a glass of water in front of each person (12 glasses for drinking). Place an empty glass in the middle of the table, and keep plenty of pitchers of water on hand for refills.

Teams alternate turns. Each player tries to bounce a quarter off the table and into the empty glass in the middle. If a player succeeds, all the players on the other team must drink their entire glasses of water. Once the glasses have been drained, refill them before moving on to the next round.

Now a player from the second team tries to bounce a quarter into the empty glass in the center. If the player succeeds, then the first team now drains their glasses. This continues until a player *has* to use the restroom, making that person's team the loser. There will be lots of squirming by the end of this game! *Michl Kohl*

Pressure-Packed Penny Game

This is a simple card game that works for a group of five or more kids. The players sit in a circle, with four pennies sitting in front of each person. The goal of the game is to avoid having the smallest card in a round. (Aces count as one and kings are the highest card.)

The dealer gives each person one card, and the player to the left of the dealer begins the game. He must choose whether to hold the card he has or exchange it with the person on his left. But beware! There are no refunds! The card received in an exchange remains with that player until the end of the round. To add some healthy tension to the game, include a three-second rule so players have three seconds or less to make a decision. Players holding kings don't have to exchange them with anyone, but if asked, they must show the cards to prove they're holding kings.

Play continues clockwise around the circle until it returns to the dealer. She may keep the card she has or take the top card from the deck. The round ends after the dealer makes her decision, then all cards are revealed. The loser is the player left holding the lowest card. As his penalty, he must toss one penny into the middle. The last person holding a penny wins the game.

If this strikes you as being too much like gambling, substitute candy for the pennies, or use other items instead of cards (such as checkers chips, chess pieces, and so on). *Joel Oesch*

Musical Baby Food

Just as it sounds, this game is played like musical chairs, but uses baby food instead of chairs. You need one fewer jars of baby food than you have players, a spoon for each player, and music to play during the game. Any number of students can play. Divide everyone into several smaller groups, or use this as a discussion starter by choosing a handful of students to play in front of the whole group. If you choose to do the latter, have the participants stand side by side so the rest of the audience can see their awesome facial expressions during the game.

When the music starts, begin handing jars of baby food to the first person in line. Start with milder flavors like peaches, pears, and bananas, but as the game goes on, introduce the nastier flavors like peas, green beans, prunes, and turkey vegetable medley. Players should pass them up and down the line until the music stops. Now anyone holding a jar of baby food must eat a great big spoonful! And the student left without a jar is out.

For each subsequent round, remove a jar of baby food and start the music again. The last person left standing with a jar of baby food is the winner—or loser, depending on how you look at it. Turkey vegetable medley? Yuck! *Rich Griffith*

Body-Part Musical Chairs

Have everyone form a big circle of chairs with the seats facing out from the center. Remove one chair and then start the music. Everyone now walks—or jogs—around the chairs until the music stops. You or another leader should call out the name of a body part. Start with simple things like nose, hair, and left elbow; then get more complicated with things like bare feet, someone else's left hand (the person to your left, perhaps), and so forth. If a player gets antsy and touches a chair before the body part is named, that player is out.

When the part is named, everyone races to touch it to a chair, but only one player per chair is allowed. The player left without a chair is eliminated. Before beginning the next round, remove another chair (or two to speed things up) and start again. The game is over when the music stops and there's only one player left touching a chair. *Troy Smith*

Truth-or-Dare Spin the Bottle

On narrow slips of paper (at least one per player), write out several different questions as well as some dares (see samples below). You may want to let your students write these up, but remind them to be tasteful and lighthearted so no one gets too uncomfortable during the game. Place the papers inside a bottle, but before you play, make sure you can easily extract them or this game will be very short and disappointing!

Have the students sit in a circle on the floor. Lay the bottle on its side in the middle of the circle and choose someone to spin first. When the bottle comes to a stop, whomever the mouth of the bottle is pointing to must take out a slip of paper, read it out loud, and then either truthfully answer the question or do the dare.

Once that's been completed, that player gets to spin the bottle and the fun starts all over again. Keep playing until all the slips have been drawn.

Here are some sample dares you can use:

1. Do your best impression of the youth pastor.
2. Reveal your most embarrassing moment.
3. Turn to the person next to you and stick your finger in that person's nose (or mouth, ear, etc.).
4. Act like a monkey with a bad case of fleas.
5. Tell your favorite clean joke.
6. Chew someone else's A.B.C. (already been chewed) gum.
7. Raise your arms and let everyone tickle you for one minute.
8. Say a funny movie quote.
9. Cling to an inanimate object, such as a tree or wall, and holler, "Someone help me—I'm stuck!"
10. For the rest of the game, holler something every time someone says something negative. *Alvin Thomas*

BOB GAME

In the original game of Concentration you slap your knees, then clap once, then snap the fingers of your right hand, then snap the fingers of your left hand. This slapping, clapping, and snapping is done by the entire group sitting in a circle. Once the group has a steady rhythm going, someone says his own name on the knee slap and someone else's name on the clap. The second person named says her own name on the next knee slap and a third person's name on the clap.

Once you've mastered playing the traditional version of Concentration, here's a trickier variation you can try with your students. Everyone sits in a circle. Choose one person to be the leader and call that person "Bob." Everyone else keeps their own names—for now.

The entire group starts a rhythm going by slapping their hands on their knees twice, then clapping twice. Keep repeating it until everyone is in unison.

Bob begins by saying "Bob" during the knee slaps and then someone else's name during the

handclaps. The person Bob names must immediately respond by saying their name during the next knee slaps and anyone's name but Bob's during the hand claps (you can't call the name of the person who just called you).

This keeps going until someone messes up. At that point the person who lost moves to the spot on Bob's right, and everyone else sitting to that person's left moves one spot to the right to fill in the hole. Here's the tricky part—the players' names stay with their original places in the circle. The ultimate goal is to unseat Bob and take his place, which is done when Bob messes up and the person to Bob's left moves right and takes Bob's place.

It's hysterical to watch kids freeze up when they forget who they are. *Dan Whitmarsh*

ELEPHANT, KAMIKAZE, MOSQUITO, BOPPITY BOP BOP BOP!

This fast-paced game will take some patient explaining and lots of practice runs to start out. The players should sit in a circle. Whoever is chosen to be "It" stands in the middle. "It" points to one person and says one of the following before slowly counting to five: "Elephant," "Kamikaze," "Mosquito," or "Boppity bop bop bop!"

When "It" says, "Elephant," the person he points to should make an elephant's snout by holding her nose with her left hand and pushing her right arm through the crook of her left elbow (see illustration). Meanwhile, the two people sitting on the sides of the elephant snout make elephant ears by touching their own heads with their outside hands. So the person sitting to the left of the middle person uses his left arm; the person on the right uses

70

her right arm. All of this must be done before "It" has finished counting to five.

Give the players a couple of chances to practice this move, and then move on to demonstrate the kamikaze move. The person pointed to should form his fingers into circles and hold them up to his eyes—like a pair of glasses (see illustration). The people beside the kamikaze make airplane wings

with their outside arms.

Now add the mosquito. The middle person makes a V with her fingers and straddles her nose with it. Then she takes the pointer finger from her other hand and sticks it through the V to resemble a mosquito's nose (see illustration). The people on either side make the mosquito's wings by holding their outside hands up to their ears, with the thumbs pointed toward their heads.

Finally, add the boppity bop bop bop part. There are no hand motions for this one. When a leader points to someone in the circle and says, "Boppity bop bop bop!" the player he pointed to must say, "Bop!" before "It" finishes saying the phrase. "It" is allowed to try to trick a player by saying only "Bop." And if the chosen player says, "Bop" back, then he's automatically "It."

If any of the three people chosen to make an elephant, kamikaze, or mosquito mess up before

"It" counts to five, then the middle player becomes "It" and the old "It" takes that person's place in the circle.

After the students get the hang of the game, "It" randomly chooses players to respond to one of the four calls. There is no set order for them. "It" should also be encouraged to gradually begin counting to five faster and faster each time to throw off the players. "It" can also add challenge to the game by calling different calls on each side of one person, who then has to use both arms to make different things.
Mike Skillman

STEAL THE TREASURE

Blindfold one person to be the guard. The guard sits in the middle of a circle of players with her noisy treasure—a set of keys, a rattle, a tin can full of change—in front of her, and a rolled-up newspaper in one hand.

Quietly choose a thief from among the remaining players. This person must try to steal the guard's treasure without making any noise. If the guard hears the thief in the act, she should start swinging her "stick" to try to stop him. If she is able to swat him with the newspaper, then he must return to his spot in the circle. However, if the thief nabs the treasure without being struck, then he becomes the new guard and a new thief is chosen for the next round. *Troy Smith*

WHO'S THE LEADER?

One person is chosen to leave the room for a few minutes. While that person is away, the rest of the group determines who will be the leader. Before you allow the missing student to reenter the room, have the leader start doing some simple actions like clapping, stomping, tapping his head, and so on. The leader should switch actions every few seconds, while the other players discreetly follow his moves so they don't give away his identity.

Now bring the student back into the room and have her stand in the middle of the circle. She gets three chances to guess who's leading the group. For subsequent rounds, choose a new guesser and leader and go again. *Troy Smith*

Zip Zap Bong!

For the most fun play this game with at least eight people, but you can play with any number of students. Have everyone stand in a circle. Tell the group that the word *zip* should be passed verbally in a clockwise motion around the circle, while the word *zap* moves counterclockwise. And when the word *bong* is said, the direction of play is reversed.

One person starts the game by saying "Zip" and "Zap" to the appropriate people next to him in the circle. Those people must respond properly or they're out and should sit down in the circle. Continue playing until only two people are left. *Troy Smith*

King of Cool

You'll get lots of laughs with this small-group game. If you have a large youth group, divide the students into smaller groups of 10 to 15 to play. At the front of the room, arrange a line of chairs side by side. You'll need one fewer chair than the number of players because one person will be standing at all times.

To begin the game, ask your players to sit down. Designate the chair on the far left as the lowest rank, Soldier #_____ (the number depends on how many total players you have), and the chair on the far right as the highest rank—or President. Between the President and the lowest ranked soldier are the ranks of Vice President, five generals (one-star through five-star), and then soldiers numbered one through however many players you have left. The person without a chair is considered "It."

The idea is for "It" to try to climb through the ranks. To do this she starts by facing off with the lowest-ranked player. The two players should stand about a foot apart and face each other with their hands behind their backs. When anyone yells, "Go!" the two players should slowly move toward each other. Whoever laughs, smiles, closes her eyes, or pushes the other player back, loses the contest. By the time they're within an inch of each other, both players should be laughing.

The student who began the game as "It" must keep trying until he at least beats the lowest-ranked player. The winner of each face-to-face contest con-

tinues to move up the ranks, while the losers sit down in their chairs. If a player loses to a soldier, that player sits in the soldier's seat.

When a player loses to a general, she must go back to the first soldier and face off with him again. If a player moves up the ranks and finally stands to face the President, she must first bow and show him respect. A presidential face-off without the bow means that player automatically loses and must go back to the beginning of the ranks. *Jae Lee*

Frozen Fish and Spoon Sewing

Originally an ancient rite of passage involving a fishing line, a frozen suckerfish, small chunks of ice, and a group of pre-pubescent youth, "Frozen Fish and Spoon Sewing" has spread like wildfire and become the hottest new activity among international youth. Yes, the game has evolved a bit, but it is still a rite of passage. Before this game, your kids will be a bunch of gangly, socially awkward teenagers—but *after* they've played, they will be a bunch of gangly, socially awkward teenagers. Well, maybe the game isn't that life-changing after all.

In preparation for your game (at least a day or two beforehand), tie one end of a long piece of string (the length depends on how many kids you have, but say 20 feet long) to a metal spoon. Now feed the next bit of string after the spoon through an ice cube tray filled with water. Put the tray, with spoon and string, into your freezer and freeze it solid. Just before playing, crack the string out of the tray so you have one really, really cold spoon with an ice cube-laced string attached. Do this process with two spoons so you now have two frozen spoons with ice cubes on two long strings.

Divide your group into two teams and have each team form a line. Turn on some wacky music and let the icy fun begin! The object of the game is to "sew" the icy spoon underneath the kids' clothing. The first person in each line sends the spoon down her shirt and pants (not inside the underwear, however). When the spoon comes out the bottom of her pant leg, then the next player takes it and sends it up through his pant leg and shirt and out the collar for the next player to take and send it down. This up-and-down process is repeated through each line so all the kids are connected by the string. The first team to have its string completely removed from every player's clothing wins!

A more disgusting option you could try is to use a real frozen fish. Choose a small kind, like smelt, although using a frozen bass might be interesting. Just drill a hole through the fish so you have a place to securely tie the string. Then add on the ice cubes as described above, or use more frozen fish instead of ice. This will give the players even more incentive to sew fast before those fish thaw! Ewww! *Marshall Allen*

ALPHABET BASEBALL

Choose a topic or category of things like animals, insects, or cars. Choose one player to start the game. Going around the circle, everyone tries to name something from the chosen category that begins with the letter A. Keep going until someone can't think of an original and appropriate item that begins with A. (There should be no repeats!) Whoever interrupts the progression of play receives a strike; if a player gets three strikes, she's out.

After the "A" round ends, the person sitting to the left of the player who started last time begins by naming something in that category beginning with the letter B. On around the circle it goes once more. Your kids will come up with things you've never heard of to try to stay in the game! *Diana Smith*

• **Encore.** First do some brainstorming with your adult volunteers and come up with some categories or words like *girl's name, boy's name, body of water, day of the week, state name,* and so forth. Write them on index cards, one category or word per card.

Split the group into smaller teams of two to eight players. Each team will choose a card and then sing (as a team) at least eight words of a song that fits the category or includes the word that is written on their drawn card. For example, for a state name they could sing "Sweet Home Alabama." Or for a boy's name they could sing "Father Abraham."

After the first team sings a song, the other teams take a turn and sing parts of other songs that also fit the current category or they'll be eliminated from that round. Play should continue until only one team is left. The last team to sing an applicable song wins the round, receives one point, and gets to choose the next category card to start round two.

Have the teams track their own points and then tally them at the end. The winning team can sing a chorus of "We Are the Champions" to finish the game.

• **First-to-Last Name Game.** One team starts with a name like Tom Cruise. Now the other team must come up with a new first name that begins with the last letter of that person's last name, like Edward Scissorhands. You can also play using song titles instead of people.

THE (CHRISTIAN) LIST

This game is based on the VH1 show called "The List," so if you can, watch a few episodes ahead of time to make sure you know how it's played. Pick four people to be the contestants and one to be the host. Give players the category beforehand so they can come prepared. The categories could be things like "Best Christian Artist," "Best Christian Song," or "Best Christian Musical Group."

Each contestant picks her top three choices in the given category. In addition, if the category is related to music, contestants could bring samples of the musical groups or songs that they chose for their top three.

To play the game, the host asks each person to share his third choice and why he chose it. (Ask a volunteer to stand somewhere up front and make a list of the players' choices on a whiteboard or overhead projector so everyone can see it.) If the students brought music samples, you could play a quick sound bite of each player's choice after she explains why she chose it. Tell the host to encourage discussion throughout the game regarding each choice.

The host now asks for contestants' second choices and explanations, then finally for their first choices and why they're their top picks. There should now be a list of 12 things at the front of the room. One at a time, each contestant is given the opportunity to strike one item from the list, and the recorder should make a line through each one as it's eliminated. The audience (your entire youth group) then gets to vote on the remaining eight items to establish their top three choices.

Plan to play two or more rounds with different groups of students and different categories for some variety. *Stacy Goebel*

LIST CRACKER

Ahead of time, compile a variety of lists that students can relate to. You can find some good ones in an almanac. For example, you might list the top 10 highest-grossing movies of all time, the top eight participation sports among high school girls, the top 10 most populated cities in the world, the top 37 youth group phrases starting with the letter X, and the top four words used in the Bible.

Divide the students into small groups (six to eight per group) and give each group a piece of paper and a pencil. Now ask the teams to name as many items as they can for each list. They'll be competing with each other to see which team can come up with the most correct answers.

After you've shared the names of all the lists you researched and given the students adequate time to work, reveal the answers. Give one point for every correct answer that's written on the *wrong* list, and three points for every correct answer that's on the right one. *Marc Zeisloft*

SHARE AND SHARE ALIKE

Create small groups of four to six students. Give each group five minutes to make a written list of things all the group members share in common. They should ask each other questions to formulate the list, such as "Do you listen to the Backstreet Boys?" or "Do you like fries from McDonald's better than Burger King?" After time is called, have the groups tally the number of commonalties. The group with the longest list should be the first to have one kid read it out loud. Give prizes for the most unusual, bizarre, or creative area of similarity. *V.C.*

21

If you have a pool table, this is a great game that is fun, quick, and challenging. The game is played with pool balls numbered one through six (set in a triangle formation, as shown, plus a cue ball.

Two players alternate shots, even after one of them puts a ball in a pocket. Players score points for the face value of any balls they knock in. A scratch doesn't nullify a made shot, but the player's oppo-

nent may then place the cue ball on either dot and shoot for any ball on the table.

The first player to score 11 or more points wins the game and takes on the next challenger. *Rod Nielsen*

THE GRACE GAME

Prepare a sheet titled "The Challenges," listing 10 challenges. Examples of challenges—

- Recite three Bible verses and their references from memory.
- List the books of the Old or New Testament by heart.
- Sing "Give Me Oil in My Lamp" while rubbing the tummy and patting the head.
- Do a 1-minute handstand while answering (simple) math questions. (You should provide these!)
- Guess the challenger's age (if you already know, that's okay).
- Do 10 cartwheels while singing "Amazing Grace."
- Have a one-minute staredown with the challenger while the two of you have a conversation like a guy proposing to his girlfriend.
- Sing "Row, Row, Row Your Boat" to a youth leader while keeping a perfectly straight face.

Also prepare three small pieces of paper per player called *life pieces*. Explain to players that this game has a winner and a loser. The winner is rewarded, while the loser is punished. The first person challenges another person in the group with one of the challenges listed. If the person challenged performs the challenge successfully, that player holds on to his life pieces. If not, he must surrender a piece to the challenger. Continue until someone has no more life pieces.

Determine who has the most life pieces, and bring the winner and the loser up to the front—the judgment seat. Take the life pieces from the winner and count them. Just when the loser is looking around nervously for some awful punishment, give the life pieces to the loser, declare her the winner, and give her the prize.

Be forewarned: The person who thought he won the game (probably your athletic or highly competitive type) is not going to be overjoyed by this turn of events. But this plays into the object of this lesson. Ask the kids questions like—

- Does the loser deserve to win?
- Is it fair?
- Is it fair that we get to go to heaven?
- Do we *deserve* to go to heaven?
- Haven't we all lost the game because we've sinned?

Get a conversation going about this. If feathers are really ruffled, you may want to point out that this game isn't a perfect comparison—no one loses out because someone else gets "their" grace. God has enough grace for everyone—every person can go to heaven. Maybe pull the winner/loser aside later, tell him you know how hard it was to see things suddenly turn around, and thank him for being a good sport (if he *was* a good sport.) *Joel Smit*

PSYCHOLOGIST

Pick somebody to be the patient, and have her choose what her psychological problem is. It can be anything from thinking she's a dog to believing she's the person next to her. Obviously her malady shouldn't manifest itself in any overt physical way, such as obsessive hand washing—that would be way too easy.

The rest of the group must ask the patient questions to determine a diagnosis. The patient can only respond yes or no. So if the question isn't in yes-no format, the patient can't answer it. It'll be hard to figure out which is funnier: the things patients decide are wrong with them or the questions your group asks out of total desperation!

THE QUESTION GAME

Challenge even your most focused kids with this fast-paced game. Divide them into groups of six or eight players. One player asks someone else in the group a question. That person doesn't answer, but asks someone else in the group a question instead. Kids are out when they—

- Answer the question just asked of them.
- Repeat a question that's already been asked.

- Hesitate more than three seconds before asking a new question.
- Ask a question of the person who just asked them (until there are only two kids left).

The last person left is the winner.

NO RULES GAME

Divide kids into groups of six to eight players—or you can play with one small group. Rule making rotates clockwise around the circle with each student creating a random rule and a consequence for breaking the rule. For example, you can't say *if*. When you do, you have to stand up and crow like a rooster for five seconds.

The group becomes self-monitoring as more rules are added, trying to catch each other breaking the rules. If a consequence sends a player away from the group—say, to interact with another group—rules continue to be created while the rule-breaker is away, increasing the chances that the returning person will break even more rules. Play ends when pandemonium ensues.

WHAT'S FOR SALE?

Pick a salesperson, who immediately leaves the room. Show the rest of your group an item (toilet brush, hammer, Pepto Bismol, barf bag), and then place it in a box or suitcase. Bring the salesperson back into the room. She tries to sell the item to the group without knowing what it is. Audience members ask questions about the item to help the salesperson identify what she's selling (for example, "Does this item work on pets?"). The salesperson must answer the questions. See how long it takes her to figure out what she's selling.

TELEPHONE CHARADES

You decide on a multiple-part situation that students can act out—jogging, getting sweaty, taking a shower, and drying off or eating, getting sick, and barfing in the toilet. The person who begins the game must be dramatic and detailed in the event he's acting out. It often works best to use an adult as the initial actor.

To begin the game get four volunteers who leave

the room, returning one at a time when they are called back into the room. Tell the audience and the lead (adult) actor what he will be acting out. Bring the first student into the room. She watches the leader perform the scene. When it's finished, the second student comes in and watches the first student imitate what she saw the leader act out. Then the third person comes in and watches the second student imitate the first student. The fourth student watches the third student act out the scene and then tries to guess what was being acted out. Only the fourth person guesses—all the others just imitate the person before them.

Song of Solomon Beauty Statements

This game can be played with individual players or with teams. Read—or pass out copies of—a list of real and bogus compliments from Song of Solomon. Have the players guess which ten are really in there! The player or team with the most correct guesses wins.

• **Parable Titles.** This game is similar to Song of Solomon Beauty Statements, but in this game you create real and bogus titles for Jesus' parables.

Warhead Face

Buy a bag of Warheads candies—a super-sour candy. Pick three or four contestants to come up front. Have them all put three candies in their mouths and see who can go the longest without showing any expression or making any noise.

Screenwriters

Choose a short video clip that is dialog-based, like the discussion between Luke Skywalker and Darth Vader in *Star Wars*. Divide your group into teams of five to eight. Explain that you're going to show a short video clip once or twice, without sound, and then give them five minutes to write dialogue for the scene.

Show the clip a couple of times. Give teams five minutes to write their screenplay. Then have them select readers to read the team's dialog while you roll the clip again. For a fun variation, give each team a theme for their dialog.

GAMES

Nothing tweaks kids, lowers barriers, or bonds youths with their youth pastor like making messes. Of course these games need to be played where you can clean up easily. No matter what surroundings you have, you'll find plenty of messy games your kids will love. Games can be combined for a theme night—The Yuck Olympics—an event that will be long remembered!

BOLOGNA FACE

Form pairs of players and have them stand about five feet apart, facing each other. Give one of the students in each pair a slice of bologna. When you say, "Go!" students should toss the lunch meat to their partners, who try to catch it with their faces. If they succeed in doing so without using their hands, then to finish the round they must eat the bologna—also sans hands.

Eliminate any pairs who don't catch the bologna or can't manage to eat it off their faces without help. Then have the remaining partners take three more steps away from each other and play again with new pieces of bologna. This time the partners trade tosser and catcher roles. Keep playing and eliminating pairs until only one remains. Give those partners what's left of the package of bologna as their prize.

Joseph Crew

YUCK CHAMBER

For your next messy event that may involve the throwing of runny, slippery, and sloppy stuff at one another, use a "yuck chamber" to help confine the mess while allowing spectators to watch the action safely and cleanly from the outside.

You'll need 12 2' x 4' x 8' pieces of wood (spruce is the cheapest) and 20 two-inch screws to construct a square frame that measures 8' x 8' x 8'. Use a staple gun to attach from the inside four (or five, if you want to add a top to the chamber) 8' x 8' sheets of plastic to the sides of the cube. To reinforce the edges, twist some plastic grocery bags and staple them on top of the edge of the plastic while stapling it to the wood. This measure will help keep the plastic from being pulled away from the wood.

On one side of the yuck chamber, make a vertical slit in the plastic to be used as an entrance and exit. Make sure the slit is reinforced with plastic packing tape and plastic bags.

You can use this see-through arena for food fights, mud wrestling, or any messy game you'd like your students to experience, if you don't want to hose down your youth room afterward. *Len Cuthbert*

Baby-Food Spoon

Two players lie on their backs, head-to-head, on top of a long table. One student feeds the other student baby food, preferably a fruit flavor that won't make the person gag. Give the feeder a spoon and a jar of baby food to spoon over her head and into the receiver's mouth. Most of the time she'll probably miss her partner's mouth, so the eater should wear a pair of goggles to protect his eyes.

A variation on this game is to give both players goggles and have them feed each other simultaneously. Either way, someone's going to have a messy face! *Monty Eastman*

No-Hands Burger-Eating Contest

Just prior to game time, buy four or five of the biggest, messiest hamburgers in town (Whoppers from Burger King, Big Macs from McDonald's, or any burger from Carl's Jr. will work). Announce to the group that you're going to have a contest to see who can eat a big, juicy hamburger the fastest, then ask for four or five volunteers.

Position your contestants in front of the crowd for optimal viewing. Have them sit behind a table, and place the burgers on top of their wrappers for them. As they anticipate the start, begin slowly counting to three. Just before you say, "Go!" tell them you forgot an important rule: They can't use their hands! The results are hilarious as the kids struggle to corral the elusive ingredients and get a face full of lettuce and special sauce.

Have an impartial judge standing by to declare the winner. The prize could be a fancy napkin, a roll of antacids, or a fast-food restaurant gift certificate. *Brian Moyer*

French Fry Fiasco

Buy 12 fast-food orders of large fries. (Twelve large orders will work for a group of about 45 students.) Place two large trash bags on the floor, and you're ready to go.

Divide the group into two teams and have each team kneel around one of the trash-bag-covered areas with their hands behind their backs. On the count of three, have two adults dump half the order of fries onto each trash bag. The first team to consume all their fries without using their hands is the winner. *Chris Edgington*

Guzzler

For each player, tape together two cans of soda so their openings are on opposite sides. The contestants will open both of their cans at the same time and see who can be the first to guzzle all the soda. If a person chooses to drink from one can first, then the other can will spill all over her. And if she tries to sip from both sides equally, be prepared for large expulsions of gas! Give the winner a six-pack of soda. *Monty Eastman*

Ice Cream Nylon Suck

Serve up a tasty treat of ice cream—one bowl per pair of players. The kids sit in chairs facing their partners. One partner holds a bowl full of ice cream and a spoon and gets ready to feed the ice cream to his partner. But first, give the eater a leg of pantyhose to pull over her head and face. Now give the signal and watch players try to suck their ice cream through the nylon! *Jayson Turner*

Sundae Relay

On a long table, place one large bowl of vanilla ice cream per team and six bowls of various sundae toppings with a few large serving spoons in each. Use crushed Oreo cookies, M&Ms, chocolate syrup, nuts, bananas, cherries, whipped cream, sprinkles, and whatever else you like on an ice-cream sundae—but make sure you have only six choices. Each topping should be clearly marked with a number, one through six.

Divide the group into teams of seven players, and ask each team to choose a captain. Give each team captain a die. Ask captains to number off their teammates, one through six. The game begins as each captain rolls the die and then sends the team member with that number to the table to add the topping with that same number to the team's bowl of ice cream. After 10 to 15 seconds, call out, "Switch!" and the captains should roll again and repeat the process.

Keep an eye on the sundaes, and call time after three to four minutes. Give awards for unique design or massive size, and then hand out spoons so teams can enjoy their creations! *Kennie and Amy Jackson*

Egg Tube-Blowing

Here's an egg game played *without* the shell. Take a three-foot-long piece of clear, plastic tubing (you can get this at Home Depot for about $5) and a dozen eggs. Crack open three to four eggs and pour the yolks and whites into the tube.

Position a student at each end, and at the count of three both should start blowing into the ends of the tube for as long as they can. After about 10 seconds or so, someone will need to take a breath and will get egg all over the face. This inexpensive stunt will have the rest of the youth group laughing and grossed out at the same time. *Adam Reynolds*

Spaghetti Stretch

Take a pound of cooked spaghetti and divide it between two bowls as equally as possible. Two teams will compete to see who can make the longest continuous line of spaghetti on the floor. Or make a finish line at the other end of the room and declare that the first team to get their line of spaghetti across the line wins.

One person on each team will be in charge of extracting the noodles from the bowl and handing them to teammates one at a time. A person who receives a noodle will lay the piece on the floor touching the last piece, and then run back to let the next player go. Once a piece of spaghetti is on the floor and the player has stopped touching it, it cannot be straightened or moved again. *Ken Lane*

Dark Room

Keep your kids guessing, and make them work for their prizes. You can use this idea during a youth meeting where you have a number of fierce competitions going on between individuals or teams.

Transform a room so it's completely dark when the lights are turned off. Hang strings from the ceiling with harmless objects tied to the ends: Nerf balls, scarves, rubber spiders, and so on. Line the entire floor with trash bags or other types of protective covering. Now in different places on the plastic, spread items that have varying textures: cotton, gravel, Jell-O, cottage cheese, and so on.

Now somewhere in the midst of all of this, place your prizes in different locations around the room. Get a good mixture of cool and cheesy prizes: two-liter bottles of soda, candy, games, Bibles, CDs, broken toys, and canned food.

Here's how it works: After a competition is finished, the winner earns a chance to enter "the dark room." If it was a team competition, ask the winning team to choose a representative or two from their group to go. The chosen students should remove their shoes and socks before you blindfold them. Send them into the dark room for two or three minutes and let them grope around for their prizes. It can be a lot of fun for kids to walk blindly into the darkness while things hit them in the head and weird textures mush and crunch under their feet. *Teresa McCasland*

Jell-O Bobbing

This game is good for all ages, but junior highers seem to love it more than older students. For each team provide a punch-size bowl of Jell-O with pieces of wrapped candy at the bottom. Make sure you have enough candy in each bowl so every player on a team will be able to retrieve a piece. Set the bowls on a long table at the opposite end of the room from your starting line.

Divide the group into even teams and line them up single file. At your signal, the first player for each group runs to his team's bowl of Jell-O, dunks his head in, and tries to come up with a piece of candy. Once he has a piece between his teeth, he runs back to tag the next person in line.

The first team to successfully retrieve all the candy from their bowl of Jell-O, even if some players have to go twice, wins. Let everyone eat their candy after the game is finished. *Troy Smith*

Jell-O Slurp

Each team gathers around a large bowl of Jell-O (any flavor). Give each player a straw to slurp the

Jell-O through. The first team to empty their bowl wins. If you have a small group, individuals can compete against one another with their own bowls of Jell-O instead. *Patty Ellis*

ROADKILL CHUBBY BUNNY

You undoubtedly know how to play the original Chubby Bunny game—players stuff jumbo marsh-mallows into their mouths one at a time until they can no longer say, "Chubby bunny." To spice up this old favorite, try dunking the marshmallows in strawberry or chocolate syrup first.

PIE OR POINTS

Separate into two teams. A player from each team is chosen to come forward. The two contestants stand on opposite sides of a table with a pie tin full of whipped cream sitting in the middle of it. The host asks the players to answer a question, and the first to respond correctly is given a choice—take the points or shove the pie in the other person's face.

The kind of questions you ask doesn't really matter. They can be biblical, about current events—whatever fits into your agenda for the meeting. Call up two more players to answer the next question, and each time the one who answers correctly must choose between taking the points for the team or putting a pie in the other person's face.

Keep a running score of points accumulated by each team. You can change the point value for right answers with each round of the game, if you like. If the point values are low enough, eventually the pie will fly. (Have plenty of towels on hand for cleanup.) And if the points involved are high but a team is too far behind in the game to make any difference, it's fun to watch a player try to decide between the pie and the points. *Ken Lane*

WHIPPED CREAM CHEESEHEAD

Even if your youth group doesn't live in Green Bay, Wisconsin, you can create some real cheeseheads with this game. Each team chooses someone to put on a pair of safety goggles before using cans of whipped cream to spray every inch of the lucky volunteer's face.

Once the faces are sufficiently covered, give each team a can of cheese balls. Line up teams a few feet away from their cream-covered targets. On your signal, the cheese balls should fly until either time or ammunition runs out. The team with the most cheese balls stuck to their creamy-faced player is the winner. *K.G.*

CONDIMENTS TWISTER

Take your youth group back to the days of LPs and rec rooms with a friendly little game of Twister. Lay out your Twister mat and smear a different condiment on each colored circle—perhaps ketchup on red, mustard on yellow, pickle relish on green, and blueberry syrup on blue? Then flick the spinner and let the fun begin! *Justin Perry*

FACE PICTIONARY

This is played like the regular game of Pictionary but with a twist. You'll need a pack of Pictionary cards, or you can make up your own. Attach two pieces of butcher paper or newsprint to a wall in your meeting room. They should be hung at head-level for your teenagers. Another way to set this up is to use a large pad of paper or a flip chart set up on an easel. The latter would facilitate quicker and easier paper changes between contestants.

Now choose whether you want to play Nose Pictionary, Tongue Pictionary, or both, pitting teams against one another—"noses" versus "tongues!" For Nose Pictionary, place some bowls or paper plates of poster paint or dark-colored pudding on a table or chair next to the drawing area. For Tongue Pictionary, place small amounts of red drink syrup in small paper cups—one for each player who will draw. In other words, it's not a good or sanitary idea to allow the students to share the same cup during Tongue Pictionary. (Note: You may want to use sheets of white construction paper for the drawing surface for Tongue Pictionary. A more porous paper is better for this version of the game.)

Now divide your students into even teams. Set up head-to-head matches at different locations around your youth room. Teams can face off on different walls. In true tournament style, the winning team from each location should be pitted against a new team in the next round. Keep competing in this way until one team is declared the champion.

Once the teams have been chosen, each group stands single file and a few feet away from their drawing area. Since the competing teams will be trying to guess the same word, each should choose a runner who will race to a leader to tell the team's answer.

When a leader says, "Go!" the first person in line runs to the wall and looks at the word on the Pictionary card (an adult should stand between the two drawing surfaces and hold the cards for the players to see). The contestants then stick either their noses or tongues into the appropriate drawing substance and, with both arms behind their backs, they use only those parts of their faces to draw the word.

To make it fair, treat all words as "All Plays." If a team guesses correctly, play stops and that team gets the point. If the guess is incorrect, that team is disqualified for that round. However, play continues between the remaining teams until a correct answer is given or the round is taking too long, in which case the correct word should be announced. Then start the next round with a new runner and contestant for each team. The team that correctly guesses the most words first wins.

This game can also be played as a relay. Choose as many Pictionary cards as you have players on each team. Divide the stack of cards in half and have two leaders stand up front to hold the cards for the competitors. When half of the students have participated, the leaders can switch stacks of cards so that each team gets the same cards, only at different times. The first team to get through all the cards and sit down in line wins 40 billion points. *Michael Schaefer and Matt Sumner*

Egg Launch

Players line up at one end of the room. Each person gets a raw egg, and the first person in line gets a basketball. Players should hold the ball with the egg resting on top so when they let go of the ball, it will bounce off the floor and launch the egg in an unpredictable direction. Place several large buckets at the other end of the room, and have them try to aim their eggs at the buckets. Or to add a little more excitement, have some human targets stand a few feet away from the egg launchers. (If you do this, let the kids know ahead of time so they can wear old clothes.) *Mike Mankin*

Spam Slam

Got some old cans of Spam sitting in your pantry? Here's a creative way to get rid of it. This game is messy. The kids might want to wear old clothes. You'll need a plastic baseball bat, cans of Spam (the number of cans is determined by the size of your group), and sheets of colored paper—a different color for each team and one sheet per batter.

Divide your group into two to four even teams. One member from each team takes a turn at home plate. The pitcher throws a ball of Spam to the batter. Once the batter has hit the Spamball, the batter runs to the outfield, finds the remnant of the Spamball that landed the farthest distance from home plate, and then marks the spot with a piece of colored paper.

When one person from each team has had an opportunity to bat, the team that hit the Spamball the farthest during a round is the winner. After everyone has batted, add up the number of wins for each team. The team that won the most rounds wins the game. *Traci Fawcett*

Fish-Run Derby

To prepare for this wacky baseball variation, buy three or four gutted fish and tape the hitting end of a couple wiffle bats together with duct tape. Divide your group into smallish teams and choose a student from each team. These students will be the first fish-hitters. Give each a bat and position them 10 to 15 feet away from their teams.

When the fish is pitched, the batter tries to hit it to a teammate in the outfield. If a batter hits the fish hard enough to reach the team, give the team 10 points. If someone on the team catches the fish before it hits the ground, that team earns 15 points. Rotate new batters into play as long as the fish hold up. At the end, hose off anyone who touched a fish during the game. *Rick Moore*

CHOCOLATE NOSE RELAY

Place a kiddie pool on top of a garbage bag or two in the center of the room and apply a ring of whipped cream or chocolate syrup—or both—around it. The relay teams should line up single file on all sides of the pool—like the spokes on a bicycle tire—and stand a few feet away.

Give the first students in line each a ping-pong ball. When you give the okay, these students should drop to their hands and knees and move the balls forward with their noses. They must push the balls to the pool and then all the way around it. Unless you want trails of chocolate and whipped cream on your floor, make sure the plastic covering extends out to each team, or else let the runners stand up before they run back to tag the next players. The first team to finish wins.

COOKIE-DUNKER RELAY

At one end of the room, each team has a bowl full of two-percent or whole milk (the thicker the better) and a pile of cookies sitting in the middle of a sheet or another protective covering. At the other end, the teams should line up single file behind a starting line.

When you give the okay, the first player in each line runs to the tarp, takes a cookie from the pile, dunks it into the bowl of milk, and eats it before running back to tag the next player. But players must do all of this without using their hands. The first team to finish gets to finish off the rest of the cookies. *Paul Arakelian*

CHEWING THE CUD

Buy some beef tongues, one per team. If you're squeamish about the possibility of *E. coli* or other bacteria, ask someone behind the meat counter about the best way to cook the meat ahead of time.

Mark a starting line, and place an orange cone or a folding chair across the room from each line of students. Each team should stand single file behind someone holding the beef tongue on a plate.

This is a no-hands relay, so at your signal, the first contestant in each line must bite into the

tongue to pick it up off the plate. Then those players should quickly walk to cones or chairs at the other end of the room, circle them, and then hurry back to their waiting teammates.

The next player in line takes the tongue from the first player, also using only their teeth, before quickly strolling down to the cone and back. The first team to finish wins. This game is so hilarious—don't forget your camera! *Ryan Meeks*

EGG-IN-GLOVE WHEELBARROW RACE

Divide players into teams of two, and give each team a pair of disposable surgical gloves and two eggs. One person will act as the wheelbarrow while her partner pushes her during the race. Line up the teams behind a starting line that stretches across the width of the youth group room. Before you start, each wheelbarrow person should put on gloves and then slip an egg onto the palm of each hand under the glove.

When you say, "Ready," the wheelbarrow people should get down on their hands and knees. When you say, "Set," the pushers should lift their partners' legs. And when you say, "Go!" they should start walking toward the finish line on the other side of the room. Obviously, they'll need to tread very carefully because they don't want to break the eggs in their hands. The first team to reach the finish line with two unbroken eggs is the winner. *Len Cuthbert*

DOUBLE WHEELBARROW FORMATION

Here's a quirky way to run your relay races that also requires a little more teamwork. Form teams of four. Two students get down on all fours, crouched side by side. Their teammates stand behind them and pick up their legs, like in the normal wheelbarrow position. However, the leg-holders don't hold one person's legs as usual; they must each hold *one* leg from each wheelbarrow person. When everyone is in position, begin your race or relay.

All kinds of relays can be done with these teams of four. Have them race to specific points in the room or out in a field; have them go through an obstacle course; or have multiple heats with team members changing positions, allowing the players on the bottom to become the leg-holders and vice versa. *Pam Malloy*

84

POPCORN-DIP RELAY

Use this game to help your students let off a little steam before a movie night. Fill some large buckets to the rim with popcorn, and line up your relay teams at the other end of the room (one team per bucket of popcorn). Have an adult use a small paintbrush to carefully apply a small amount of honey to the runners' faces.

Honey-faced players should run and plunge their faces into their teams' tubs of corn and then run back to tag the next players in line. It doesn't matter which team finishes first, but whoever brings back the most pieces of popcorn stuck to their faces wins. *Monty Eastman*

PANCAKE-BATTER RELAY

Mix up a five-pound bag of flour with lots of water. You want a runny mixture for this game. Pour the batter into five-gallon buckets (one per team), filling each bucket half full. Line up teams of five to 10 players and place a bucket of batter at one end of the line and an empty one-gallon (or smaller) bucket at the other. If you plan to play this indoors, place a large sheet of plastic under the buckets and the players.

The first player on each team scoops out some batter with his hands. Then the players pass the batter down the line—hand to hand—until it reaches the last person on the team, who then dumps what's left into the smaller bucket. Teams repeat the process until the smaller container is filled. The first team to fill their empty bucket to the rim wins. *Ken Lane*

KISS MY FEET

Mark a starting line at one end of the room. At the other end, make a line of chairs with three or four feet between chairs. Place a paper plate full of Hershey's Kisses on each chair. Create relay teams with even numbers of students so they can pair off. If one team comes up a member short, one of their players should go twice.

Each team should line up directly across the room from one of the chairs. Before you start the race, have all the players remove their shoes and socks. At the signal, the first pair of players on each team runs to that team's chair. One student must grab a Kiss, unwrap it, and put the candy into her partner's mouth, using only her toes. As soon as the Kiss has been swallowed by the player, it's that person's turn to feed his partner in the exact same way. After each partner has eaten a Kiss, the two run back and tag the next two players. The first team to finish wins. *Rex Hunter*

PB AND J SANDWICH RACE

Make your starting line. At the other end of the room, set up a line of chairs(one for each team(and space them about three feet apart. Place a loaf of bread, a bowl of peanut butter, and a bowl of jelly on the floor in front of each chair (leave the bread bag untied so the players can retrieve the bread slices easily and quickly). Also place a towel and some hand wipes to one side of each chair.

Create some relay teams of six guys and six girls each, and have teams line up boy-girl-boy-girl. You can use smaller teams if necessary but make them coed if possible. At your signal, the first guy-girl pair from each team runs to that team's chair. The girl sits down and the guy takes off the girl's socks and shoes. Now the female contestant must make her partner a peanut-butter-and-jelly sandwich with her feet, and then he has to eat it.

After the guy has swallowed the last crumb, he runs back to tag the next pair while the girl moves to the side and cleans off her feet—hopefully without leaving a trail of peanut butter and jelly across the floor. Once a girl's feet are clean, she should put her shoes and socks back on and go sit with her team.

The first group to have all their players finished and sitting in line wins. Offer the winning team some peanut-butter-and-jelly sandwiches made the way their mothers used to make 'em—with knives. *Joshua Ater*

FOOT ID

You'll get some great reactions with this game. Place food items such as pizza, tuna fish, potato chips, cottage cheese, and cat food in six different shoebox-size containers (one kind of food per container). Use your imagination when choosing the food items—the crazier the better!

Ask for six volunteers to come forward and sit in a line of chairs that faces the audience. Ask each volunteer to remove the shoe and sock from one foot, then blindfold all the volunteers. Get six more volunteers to come up and assist the players. Each helper will need a sheet of paper and a pen or pencil to use during the game.

Place a container of food at the feet of the first player. Have her stick her foot inside and try to identify what the food is. When she has a guess, ask her to whisper it to her helper, who will record her answers on the paper for later scoring.

Keep the food moving. Once player one has made a guess, pass the first container of food down the line so player two can also guess. Meanwhile, go ahead and give player one the second container of food to identify. Do this over again until every foot has had a chance to feel every food. When everyone is finished, hand out warm, wet washcloths and towels to the contestants so they can clean their feet.

Share the correct identity of the food in each container, and ask the helpers to tally up each player's score so you can announce a winner. *Ken Lane*

GAUNTLET

Play this game in a tiled hallway or another uncarpeted area that's about nine feet wide by 20 feet long. Lay down some sheets of plastic or tape together some trash bags and tape them securely to floor to protect it. Now that you've made your runway, carefully scatter raw, unbroken eggs all over the plastic, keeping them two to three feet away from the edges.

Each player should remove one shoe and sock and wear a blindfold to play this game. The object is to hop on one foot (the bare one) from one end of the plastic to the other without landing on an egg, hopping off the plastic, or touching the walls. A leader or fellow student should stand at the finish

YUCK

According to the Rec FX Web site, www.recfx.com, YUCK™ is a unique recreation product that provides slime without the slime and mess without the mess. It simply replaces the need for using gelatin, mud, food, or other messy substances for activities or games." A one-pound jar of Yuck can be purchased from Rec FX for about $12. Check out their site or call toll-free 877-367-3239 for current prices and more information about this amazing product.

line and shout instructions to each player about where to hop next.

If a player lands on an egg, that person is out. Have some wet washcloths and towels handy to clean up the losers' feet before they step out of the area. Cover the smashed eggs with paper towels before the next player goes. If a player should hop onto a paper towel, it doesn't count as an egg smash. It just saves time if you don't stop to clean up the smashed eggs between players.

Time all the players who successfully complete the course and then reward the student who finishes with the best time. *Shawn Swinney*

SPOON DIGGING

Prepare a large bowl of chocolate pudding with a combination of whole prunes and strawberries mixed in. You'll also need a plastic spoon for every pair of players. The players will compete against the clock in this game.

On your signal, the first pair runs to the bowl with their spoon. Then one player places the spoon handle in her mouth and, without using her hands, digs out a blob of pudding that contains either a prune or a strawberry. She feeds the fruit to her partner—still no hands—and after it's been chewed and swallowed, the pair runs back to the starting line and their time is recorded. The team that accomplishes this feat the fastest is the winner. You can also have two teams race against each other.

This game is sure to produce some splattered faces, as well as grimaces whenever players bite into chocolate-covered prunes! *Brian Moyer*

FOOD SLIP 'N SLIDE

Have some summertime fun with an edible twist. Make your old Slip 'N Slide (or a sheet of plastic) slippery with the makings of a meal. For breakfast use powdered pancake mix, syrup, and eggs (the kids will really stink afterward if you use this game in the heat of the day).

Good lunch or dinner items include cans of sloppy joe mix, fruit cocktail, pork and beans, and chicken noodle soup. Finally, for dessert you can use chocolate syrup, chopped peanuts, whipped cream, rainbow sprinkles, and cherries.

Use your imagination, and try anything that's easy to spread but won't burn the kids' eyes or skin, like hot sauce, mustard, vegetable oil, and so on. *Tyson Behrns*

MISSION: DISGUSTING!

Use plastic to cover the floor, walls, and anything else that could get messy. Tape lengths of string at different heights above the plastic, and pull them tight so they're taut. The strings should cross over each other like laser beams.

Now mix up some nasty combinations of stuff to create a really gross, slimy, and stinky substance; then spread it all over the plastic. Students should wear old clothes and bring spare outfits to change into after playing this game.

Players line up at one end of the plastic. One at a time they must get to the other side of the plastic without touching the strings. If they touch the strings, they're out. When you set up your playing area, make it so they'll have to crawl across to reach the other side, and will often have to slide underneath the strings on their stomachs—right through that nasty stuff. No player is allowed to go across on feet or toes.

Time each player's attempt, and then let the players get cleaned up before you give an award for the fastest time. *Shawn Swinney*

VIDEO ANNOUNCEMENTS

To add zip to your announcements of upcoming events, take to the streets with your camcorder and record strangers making each announcement. The possibilities are endless: checkout clerks at a grocery store, high school football teams, young people coming out of a theater, Wal-Mart shoppers, the drive-through attendant at McDonald's, the pizza delivery guy, or junior high students during their lunch hour. Be creative—this can be loads of fun for you and your kids!

STEAL THE COW TONGUE

Get a giant Slip 'N Slide and purchase a real cow tongue. This game is similar to Steal the Bacon. Divide your kids into two equal teams, and have them line up across from each other on the Slip 'N Slide. The cow tongue, obviously, will be the bacon out in the middle of the Slip 'N Slide. Number each team member from one to whatever so that each person on one team has a corresponding number with someone on the other team. Now call out a number, and the player from each team with that number runs out and tries to grab the cow tongue and run back to his or her line without being tagged by the opponent. Watch the contortions and gross-out expressions as players fight to reach the cow tongue first—some won't even want it! *Tom Kopp and Tammi Cooke*

JELL-O TWISTER

Take several Twister floor sheets outside, and lay them on the grass. Throw a lot of Jell-O on each one, making sure you have more to add as the games progress. Then play Twister as you normally would, following the directions that come with the game. Hilarious! *Ellen Eisele*

MESSY RELAY

Warn kids ahead of time to wear old clothes for this game. Inflate a kiddie pool, and fill it with something icky such as Jell-O, chocolate syrup, or ketchup. Place four buckets at an equal distance from the pool. Divide the kids into four teams, and line them up between their buckets and the pool. Have them fill a deep tray from the pool (use a really poorly balanced container as a tray so there's maximum chance for sloshing), pass it overhead to the other end of the line, and empty it into the bucket. Once a tray makes it to the bucket, have the person at that end of the line move up to the pool with the tray and start again—you don't want anyone missing out on getting messy. The idea is to empty the pool into the buckets. Use your judgment as to when players are messy enough—add more to the pool if anybody's still clean. When the pool's empty, pick up the hose, spray somebody, and clean up!

GREASY SLIDE RELAY

Divide players into several equal relay teams. For this game you'll need a set of "Grandma's clothes" or other ridiculous outfit for each team. Place a large tarp on a nice grassy slope—not too steep—and grease well with Crisco or cooking oil. Teams line up at the bottom of the hill. The first person on each team races to put on Grandma's outfit and climb the tarp to the top. Then they slide back down and give the clothes to the next person in line. It's easy to adjust the difficulty of this game by finding steeper or more level slopes. The first team to have each member dress in the clothes and go up and down the slide wins.

For a great variation on this idea, find a really steep slope and have the kids "ladder." Have them lie down and build on top of each other, with the last few being pulled to the top of the tarp by their teammates. If you want to just have fun, not compete, have one team do this at a time. Teams waiting in turn have a ball watching their friends falling all over the place! *Nate Hinton*

FACE PLANT RELAY

For this game, you'll need a big stack of paper plates, a folding table or two, plate covers, and four messy substances. Decide how many teams you'll have. Set up the folding tables and place four plates for each team. Now put one of your icky substances on each plate—maybe whipping cream on one plate, applesauce on another, coleslaw or shredded carrot salad on a third, and cottage cheese on the fourth. These are just examples—go wild! Now put a plate cover over every plate. And last but not least, set up four clean-up stations nearby.

When your unsuspecting youth group shows up, divide them into your preplanned teams. Line them up close enough to the tables to see what the icky substances are once the covers are removed, but far enough away that they can't crowd the contestants. The first member of each team comes forward and stands in front of a plate. There's a moment of suspense—milk it for all it's worth!—then the cover is removed, and the player must plant his face in whatever is on the plate. Then it's off to the clean-up station with him. Send each player of each team through. End this evening of spa facials with candy or other yummy eats.

MESSY MUSICAL CHAIRS

Tell the kids ahead of time to wear old clothes. Before they arrive, set up a normal game of musical chairs. Now go around and put gross stuff on each chair. Put chocolate syrup on one chair, mustard on another—use an egg or a tomato, ketchup, pancake syrup, and so on. Be creative!
A fun addition to this messy game is to use funky music. Play music so old the kids will laugh at it (in other words, the stuff their parents listened to as teenagers!). Or use an album of theme music from comedy movies the kids will recognize. Put on "Pink Panther" and The Elephant Walk."
Give the winner a drizzly chocolate sundae on the spot (we recommend this player wash hands!). Watch the kids watching the winner eat—then take pity on 'em and make sundaes for everybody.

OUTDOOR GAMES
FOR LARGE GROUPS

These games are geared for groups of 30 or more playing in wide-open spaces. No matter how large your group is or what limitations of terrain you face, you'll find contests and activities that will work for you.

UNO BASEBALL

Set up your playing area like a standard baseball diamond. Remove all the numbered cards from a deck of Uno cards, leaving only the Skip, Reverse, Draw Two, Wild, and Wild Draw Four cards. You can play this game with the rules and equipment for either baseball or kickball.

As each batter approaches the plate, she draws a card from the pile but shouldn't reveal it to the opposing team. The Skip card lets the batter skip any base she chooses. The Reverse card requires her to run the bases in reverse order—third, second, first, home. When a player picks the Draw Two card, she runs all the bases normally, but with the batter who was on deck (next in line). A Wild card allows the batter to run the bases in any order she chooses—third, first, second, and then home; or second, third, home, back to first; and so on. Finally, a Wild Draw Four card also means a runner can run the bases in any order she chooses. However, after she gets a hit, she yells, "Come home!" and any of her teammates who are on base can run directly to home plate to score runs.

There is no limit to the number of players who can stand on a particular base at one time. Stealing bases is allowed, but only after the pitch. Once the runner leaves a base, he cannot return to it but must continue on to the next one. *Craig Butler*

BOBBYBALL

You can play this crazy game baseball-style with a fat bat and a Nerf ball, or like kickball with a playground ball. Set up the path of your bases in a zigzag pattern, and make the home plate or finish line between two orange safety cones at the end (see diagram).

Number off your students into equal teams, and flip a coin to see which team will bat or kick first. Every team bats through their entire order each inning. Outs only stop a player from scoring points. Even if a batter misses the ball, she still runs to first base. This can be an effective strategy to advance runners. However, runners don't *have* to advance, and there is no limit to how many players may occupy each base. When the ball reaches the pitcher, all runners must return to the last bases they touched, no matter where they are along the base path.

A player is out when he's tagged, he's hit below

the shoulders with the ball, or his ball is caught out of the air (just like in baseball). Every ball is playable. There are no foul balls. The fielding team may spread out all over the playing field; however, only one player may stand behind the batter. Fielders interfering with a runner on the base path will reward the runner with one extra base.

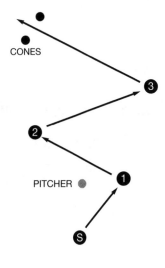

A player receives one point for each base touched and two points when crossing the finish line, making a total of five points per player possible. Players left on base at the end of the batting order receive points for the bases they already touched. So the runner standing on third base receives three points, and so on.

Play as many innings as you like. The team with the most points wins. *Jon Furman*

CHICKEN-BUCKET BALL

On a large playing field, place a five-gallon bucket at each end (see diagram). Each bucket goal should have a five- to six-foot-diameter safe zone around it. These areas cannot be guarded or entered by any team member.

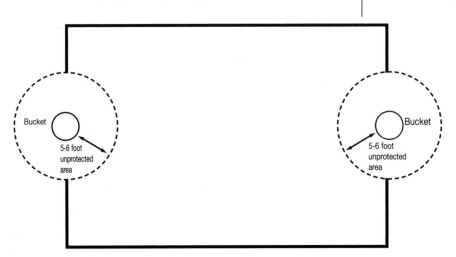

Two teams play each other using the rules of Frisbee Football or Ultimate Frisbee, but using a rubber chicken instead of a Frisbee. Each team must get its plastic poultry into the opposing team's bucket, and the chicken must be *passed* up and down the field, not thrown. Whoever is currently holding the chicken can't move until she's passed the chicken to a teammate. The opposing team may intercept the chicken and take possession at any time.

Ring a cowbell to begin the game and again whenever a point is scored. After someone makes a bucket, throw the chicken back into play and resume the game. *Dave Hirschler*

TOUCHDOWN FRISBEE

You need 10 or more Frisbees and a large rectangular playing field. Create a five- to 10-foot-wide neutral zone across the center of the field, where points cannot be scored (see diagram). This will prevent play-

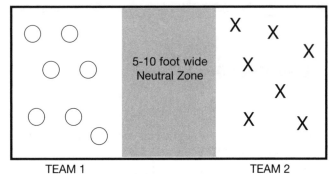

ers from slam-dunking the Frisbees in an attempt to score. Split the group into two teams and divide the Frisbees evenly between them.

The object of the game is for each team to remain on their side of the field and to throw the Frisbees into the other team's territory so they'll touch the ground before an opposing player catches them or knocks them out of bounds. If a Frisbee touches down in the neutral zone, it doesn't count. Choose a couple of adult referees to watch the action and track the teams' scores. At the end of the game, the team with the fewest Frisbee hits on their side is the winner. *Eric Robinson*

BODY-ALARM ANTICS

Many women carry body alarms that put out a shrill, deafening noise to draw attention to them when they're in danger. One of these alarms can make a great youth ministry programming device, when used in moderation:

• Use it in place of a whistle.

• Use it to silence a room full of rowdy students.

• Use it to signal the end of an outdoor game like Capture the Flag or Sardines.

• Use it on a retreat to terrify a group of junior high guys who are executing a raid on one of the girls' cabins.

• Use it to keep kids behind closed doors during camp or retreats.

• Use it with a sign on your office door that reads, "Do not open door! Alarm will sound!" and then ask the church secretary to bring something into your office. *Rick Mumford*

MOTION-DETECTOR ALARM GAMES

A few body alarms have some extra features like flashlights and motion detectors. One simple motion-detector game is to offer an award to any student who successfully picks up the motion detector and places it on his head without sounding the alarm.

Or use it like a "hot potato" and have small groups of students sit in a circle and carefully pass the alarm by the pin (or the string that's attached to the pin). If it isn't passed with great care, the pin will fall out and the alarm will sound.

To speed up the process and increase the chances of the alarm sounding, turn on some fast-paced music. Whoever is caught holding the alarm when the music stops has to do something wacky and embarrassing in the middle of the group's circle. And whoever tossed the alarm to that person can decide what she has to do—cross her eyes and stick out her tongue, do a silly dance, stand on her head, anything within reason and good taste, of course. *Rick Mumford*

NOODLE HOCKEY

Cut several eight- to 10-foot-long foam pool noodles into two- to three-foot lengths. They come in a variety of colors, so one team could use all the same color noodle sections. Use two folding chairs set five to six feet apart on each end of the field for the goals.

Create two teams, and arm each player with a section of noodle to use like a hockey stick during the game. To begin, throw a wiffle ball in the air midfield and let the teams go at it. During the game, each team must defend their goal and try to hit the wiffle ball through their opponent's goal. A player may not hit the ball with a noodle more than twice in a row. This stops a hotshot player from hogging the ball. Also, players can't touch the ball with anything other than their noodles (in other words, no kicking or hitting the ball down with their hands).

However, there are a couple of exceptions to this last rule. For example, a player will have to touch the ball after a team shoots it past the goal. To put the ball back into play, someone on the other team must toss it into the air and hit it with a noodle. And after a team scores, the other team must bring the ball back out to midfield to begin play again.

If the ball is down at the other end of the field, it's legal for players in the backfield to whack their opponents with their noodles, provided they aren't vicious about it. No whacking the head or face, though. The whacks sound awful but are virtually painless.

The game can end after a certain length of time has passed or a predetermined number of goals have been scored. This is an exhausting game, but it works for all age levels and for any size group. If you have 50 or more players, divide the group into four teams. Then alter the setup by making sticks out of four different colors of noodles and creating four goals on a square playing field instead of two on a rectangular field. Just as in the two-team competition, whichever group scores the most goals during the game is the winner. *Doug Pittam*

MURDER THE SNOWMAN

After a good snowfall, take your students outside and try this game on a large playing field set up like the diagram below. Divide into two teams and give teams some time to create their snowmen. Give equal numbers of carrots to the teams, one per player. (Before it's over, you may need as many as five or six carrots for each player.) Each player's objective is to stick a carrot into the opponent's snowman and score a point for the team. Leave the carrot in the snowman once it's stuck there. You may need an adult to monitor this in case players remove their opponents' carrots from their snowman.

When the signal to begin is given, players move from their sides of the field into the open area. No

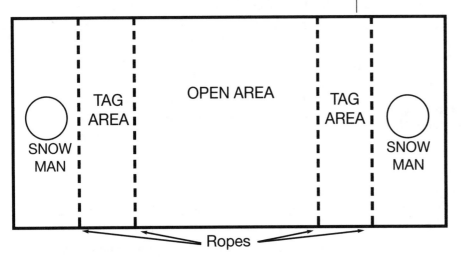

one may leave the team's area without a carrot. And carrots cannot be stashed in pockets or other hiding places—they must be visible in players' hands at all times.

Each player tries to get to the opponent's snowman on the far side of the enemy's tag area (see diagram). And he must do so without getting touched by a carrot. If a player is tagged with carrot, he surrenders his own carrot to the tagger and leaves the field to get another one. Once he has a new weapon in hand, he must return to his own tag area and start again.

To vary the game a little bit, you can move the teams' tag areas closer to each other. Or spread them farther apart and play the game in a Capture-the-Flag mode. Another variation would be to allow players to challenge one another in the open area. A

player does this by tagging a student from the other team and calling a challenge. Both players hold out their carrots. The challenger tries to break her opponent's carrot by repeatedly batting it with her own. The loser who ends up with a broken carrot must go get a new one before resuming play.

For a fun twist, award extra points at the end of the game to the team that shows the most artistic genius in decorating the opponent's snowman with carrots.

If you live where it doesn't snow or would like to play this game in a warmer season, use hay bales and old clothes to make scarecrows instead of snowmen.

Keith Turner

RUSSIAN SOCCER

Kids need to dress warmly for this one. You need a playing field with snow on it—preferably undisturbed snow. The goals should be four to five feet wide, but no more. Set the goals 30-50 yards apart from each other. You don't need any other boundary lines unless you want to create some. Depending on the number of players you have, use at least two soccer balls, but no more than four because it gets too crazy.

Tell the youth group that this game is a cross between professional wrestling, rugby, soccer, football, and insanity. Play girls against guys, and the rules are simple—guys can tackle each other, girls can tackle guys, but guys aren't allowed to tackle girls. Instead, guys can move girls away from the goal area by carrying them and gently setting them down elsewhere.

Players can throw, kick, and do whatever else is necessary to move the ball toward the other team's goal, but they must not hit, punch, or deliberately hurt other players. Station an honest person at each goal to keep score. If your adult leaders have lots of energy, get in there with them and have some fun!

Barry Yanitski

SAVING PRIVATE HERBERT

The main idea of this game is to terminate the other team's "Herbert" while protecting your own. First obtain a large quantity of pantyhose and cut the legs off. Toss the torso, keep the legs. You'll also need a large amount of flour.

Put a cup of flour in the foot of each nylon, and give the nylon legs to the students. Divide the kids into at least two teams, but more teams are better if you've got a large group of kids. Each team chooses a captain and a Herbert. (The Herberts are the only players without weapons.) Take an extra length of hose and loosely tie the captain and the Herbert together at the ankles, allowing at least three feet between them for easy movement.

Send the teams to opposite ends of a large, open playing area. Each team sends a few players out to charge the other team while some stay back to protect the captain and Herbert. Players swing their weapons to try to hit the enemies—but no head-shots. Make sure the kids hold the hosiery at the end farthest from the flour-filled toes to prevent injury; otherwise they sting like paintballs when they hit.

When people are tagged with flour, they report to a referee (that is, an adult who doesn't want to play) who can make them do something goofy before returning to the game. If the captain is hit, she must lie down where she is. Herbert, however, is still in the game and can drag the captain around or have teammates help carry the captain in order to escape. Once a Herbert is hit, the game is over and the other team is victorious.

Refill the weapons as needed and play again. Have some people filling extra lengths of hose during the game to save time. Refills are free. At the end, have a free-for-all where no one gets terminated. *Chad Wintringham*

SOCK 'EM CLEAN!

Here's a new and improved way for your students to hit their friends, fellow students, and adult leaders with some good and messy ammunition. Instead of putting flour in a sock, use shaving cream. Simply slide the sock over the can of shaving cream and press the button. As it fills, the sock will actually blow up like a balloon. You can get four or five good whacks with just one filling, and it won't hurt, but the shaving cream will fly everywhere! *Rich Griffith*

MUD CAMOUFLAGE

If you're looking for a cheap and easy way to provide uniforms for a summer afternoon of competitive outdoor games, create a big mud hole and ask all participants—even adult staff members—to jump in and cover themselves from head to toe. Be prepared for the screams and looks of disgust when you first explain what the mud hole is for. After the first brave soul dives in, the rest are sure to catch the enthusiasm. (To prevent a backlash from angry parents or a boycott from students wearing their nicest clothes, ask the kids to wear old clothes to this event.)

You may wish to divide into teams using the old shirts and skins categories. If so, ask the boys to remove their T-shirts before they dive into the muck. The real fun will come in when students try to identify their teammates underneath all that mud!

Award penalty points to players who leave any areas of skin, hair, or clothing uncovered, then deduct those points from their team's overall score. Most importantly, make sure you have buckets of clean water and garden hoses on hand to clean them all up at the end of the day! *Eben Geldenhuys*

ULTIMATE SOCK DODGE

At each end of a rectangular playing field, use orange safety cones to outline a circle that's about 10 feet in diameter. Divide the group into two teams and have each team choose a human target to stand inside its circle. The object is for players to hit the other team's human target by throwing an old gym sock filled with flour. (Have a second sock full of flour ready to go, just in case.)

The rules are the same as for Ultimate Frisbee. Players advance the sock by throwing it to their teammates. Only three steps are allowed before a player must pass the sock. If a player is cornered by an opponent, that player has five seconds to pass the sock. Defensive players are allowed to pressure the offense, but they can't touch the sock thrower. If the sock hits the ground, possession switches teams regardless of who touched it last.

Human targets can dodge the sock however they like, but they must stay within their circles. No other players may enter the target areas. Five points

POOR MAN'S EARTH BALL

Want a cheap, durable substitute for an earth ball? Purchase—or otherwise scare up—two full-size sheets and sew them together wrong side out, except for one corner that you'll leave open to stuff the sheets. Use rubber bands to tie up the three corners you've already sewn—so the ball will look round when you're done. Now turn the sheets right side out.

Blow up about 250 nine-inch balloons and stuff the sheets full. (You can get the kids to help you blow up the balloons by running a competition between teams and offering candy as prizes.) In addition, you can double-bag garbage bags and blow them up—maybe with a pump—to fill more space in the sheets. Duct tape makes an airtight seal.

When finished stuffing, close the hole with duct tape—or lace it shut with shoelaces so you can open and close it. This ball works for almost all the earth ball games, weighs less, and costs a lot less!

A fun variation on this idea is to use twin sheets to make a cylinder-shaped ball. For a giant ball, use king-size sheets. *Heath Kumnick*

---

are scored whenever a team's target is hit. Select a couple of adult referees to keep an eye on the action and track each team's points. The team with the most hits on their opponent's target wins. The flour really flies as players attempt to catch or dodge the sock. Your kids will be pretty white after this one!

Gary Noble

ULTIMATE EARTH BALL

For your goals, set up two folding chairs 10 to 15 feet apart at each end of a large playing field. Divide the teenagers into two groups and have each group choose a goalie. The rules for this game are basically the same as Ultimate Frisbee, except you use a giant playground ball. (See box above to make your own ball.)

When playing offense, team members pass the ball back and forth while running toward their opponent's goal. However, players may not run with the ball. Once they catch it, they can only pivot and pass the ball. Meanwhile, the defensive players may try to intercept the ball.

Once the ball is passed through the goal, a point is scored if it touches the ground. But if the goalie catches it first, no point is awarded. Play a certain length of time or until a desired number of goals have been scored. *Eddie Mullins*

POLE BALL

Set up two volleyball standards on opposite ends of a rectangular playing field with clear boundary and midline markings. The object of the game is to push, throw, or shove a 36-inch-diameter ball across the field until it touches the opposing team's pole to score a goal.

Each team will have players on offense and defense. The defensive players must stay on their half of the field to defend their pole. The offensive players stand on the opposing team's side of the field and cannot cross over the center line. Players cannot run with the ball and must therefore cooperate by passing the big ball around the field. Use basket-

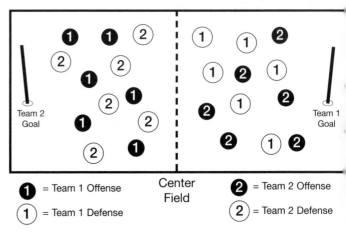

ball rules to limit body contact and prevent injury and mayhem.

Start the game with a jump ball midfield. After each goal is scored, play is resumed with another jump ball or face-off. If the ball goes out of bounds, the other team gets the ball and throws it in from out of bounds.

Give one point every time the ball touches a pole. The team with the highest number of points at the end of the game wins. *Gary Ridge*

TEAM FOUR SQUARE

Set up the foursquare box on a parking lot, making the individual squares 10 feet wide or larger, depending on how many people will stand in each.

The game is played like regular foursquare—teams try to advance to the fourth square and stay there as long as possible. People in the fourth square start each play by serving the ball underhanded to any other square. The ball must bounce once in each square. Teams hit the ball back and forth until the people in one of the squares misplays the ball and they're eliminated. Then everyone moves up to the next square, making room for a new group of people to enter the game on square one.

For a little variation, play the game with a heavy-duty, 36-inch ball and two or three players to a square. You still play the game like regular foursquare, except teams can hit the ball twice inside their own squares before bouncing it to another team. The larger ball can make some line calls difficult, so have someone serve as a judge or referee. *Allen Pickett and Henley Carson*

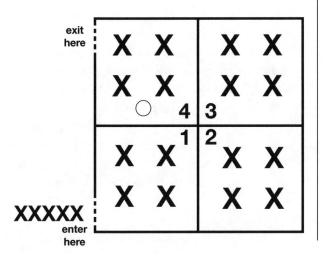

FOUR-CORNER THRASHKETBALL

The object of this chaotic, fast-paced game is to put the ball into your opponent's goal as many times as possible while protecting your own goal. Set up the playing area as shown in the diagram below. You can either make each goal with a hula hoop and two six-foot-long pieces of lumber (see illustration), or just use a large trashcan.

Divide your group into four teams of 10 or more players and assign each team a different color of beach ball. Each team should choose a goalie, who will remain within the goal area during the game. Give the teenagers one minute to find a spot on the playing field. This is where they'll stand throughout the game. Position adult leaders around the perime-

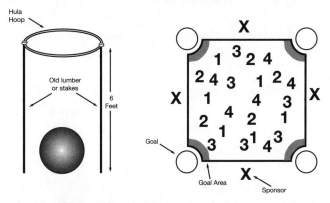

ter of the playing area to keep the ball in play and keep score for each team.

The team with the fewest number of goals scored against them wins. If you end with a tie, clear everyone from the field except those two teams and give them two to three minutes to see how many goals they can score on each other to break the tie. *Phil Morgan*

LASER TAG FOR ALL OCCASIONS!

This is a time-tested event. If you want to play laser tag one night, you can go to a professional laser tag place and drop $25 on one night of fun. But if you want to play over and over—with leaders, on retreats, during events, on weekends, and with small groups—get all the kids on the bus and take them to Wal-Mart. They sell a laser-tag set that includes the chest harness and laser gun for about $15. Toy stores carry them too. The kids buy their own sets and supply their own batteries and—voilà!—years and years of laser-tag fun!

Laser tag is simple. Each set has a gun that shoots an infrared beam (like the beam used by television remote controls) that can tag the chest or headgear worn by another player. It's a great way to spice up some old youth group games. The possibilities are endless! Check out these ideas:

• **Laser-Tag Elimination.** This is the most basic of laser-tag games. The goal is to "laser tag" the other players before they tag you. Everyone runs around the church in the dark—after you've put away all the tables and chairs, of course. It's basically all players for themselves. When a player has been hit or tagged 10 times, his laser-tag set shuts off and he's eliminated. The last player standing wins.

Or play the team-elimination version. Two teams play against each other, and the first to eliminate all its opponents wins.

• **Laser-Tag Capture the Flag.** While you're trying to capture your opponents' flag, tag 'em out with laser-tag equipment instead of your hands!

• **Sardines Laser Tag.** One person—or "It"—hides, and everyone tries to find It. The first person to find It must try to join It in the hiding place while avoiding being tagged out by It's laser gun. It shouldn't be too hard, since it takes 10 shots to tag someone out. But woe to the people who find the sardines last, for they could have 10 or 20 laser guns shooting at them at once! They can shoot back at the sardines, but the sardines will keep shooting until they've been hit 10 times themselves, which is unlikely.

• **Laser-Tag Kick the Can.** "It" tries to tag players before they can kick the can. But who's to say It has to tag people with a hand? We're in a new millenium! Tag 'em with a laser gun instead!

• **Laser-Tag Run the Gauntlet.** Take all the laser-tag chest harnesses and put them on one person—all over the person's body. Everyone else forms two straight lines that face each other. The goal is for the person wearing all the chest harnesses to run between the two lines of players without any of the harnesses shutting off.

If you have fewer than 40 people in your group, the chest harness person will probably have to run several laps before a harness terminates. So you might say, "Okay, Sally, you've got to make it to that wall and back three times without any of the chest harnesses terminating."

• **Laser-Tag Flag Football.** Play a regular game of flag football, but instead of pulling the flags from your opponents, tag 'em with your laser gun to stop the play.

FOOD CHAIN

This game works best with 30 to 40 players. With this size of group, choose one student to be a bear, three to be wolves, three to be owls, and arbitrarily declare various remaining students to be mice, squirrels, and rabbits in roughly equal numbers.

Explain that this game is like tag except that it's a night and day game. When you call day, the wolves hunt owls, mice, squirrels, and rabbits (these particular owls sleep on the ground). When you call night, owls hunt wolves, mice, squirrels, and rabbits (these wolves can be killed in their sleep). The bear hunts everybody all the time. When a mouse, squirrel, or rabbit is caught (tagged) by a predator, she is dead.

If you decide to play this indoors, douse the lights for night. If outdoors, make sure everyone can hear you when you call night and day. Since you created predators—bears, wolves, and owls—in proportion to the size of your group, count the predators. When there's an equal number of prey (mice, squirrels, and rabbits) surviving, the game is over and the prey get to be the new predators. *Brian Stegner*

AMBUSH

Here's a fun option to tag along with other games when you're using teams or small groups of kids. Every so often, without warning, youth leaders ambush a group and tie them all together in a mass. They must continue the activity in this way for as long as you decide. Keep watch over the groups so no one gets an unfair advantage due to other teams being tied up. At the end of the games, tie the groups together in a big wad and have them eat brownies—but they can't feed themselves. *Heather Shrum*

FOR SMALL GROUPS

The name of *this* game is adaptability. Some of these games require large outdoor spaces like an open field, but most games can be tweaked to work with your existing space. Many games can also be adapted for large groups. You have plenty of options for fun and action here.

GLOW-IN-THE-DARK KICKBALL

Purchase a large, semi-transparent rubber ball. You can get one at Target or Wal-Mart for about $3. Make sure you get one that has a plug in it, not just an inflation valve. The opening has to be large enough for you to insert narrow objects into the ball. (Sometimes they come with plastic spiders, ants, flies, and so forth inside them.) Pull the plug out of the ball, crack open three glow sticks (you can get these for $1.50 to $2.00 apiece), and pour the glowing substance into the ball. Re-inflate the ball and replace the plug.

Play a normal game of after-dark kickball in an open area, using the glowing ball. To spice it up even more, mix it up every other inning by making the players run the bases backward or kick and run with partners. *Keith Morgan*

MUSHBALL

This game is a combination of tennis and baseball. It's a great tool for teaching your students about humility. Before you play, get a medium-size wiffle bat and turn it into a "mushbat." Cut off the hitting end and stuff newspaper inside. Wrap some duct tape around the bat until you've covered it about

three times. This deadens it. You also need a tennis racket, a softball with some weight to it, and four bases (like those used for games of baseball or kick-ball).

Choose two team captains and give them a few minutes to choose players for their teams. Make sure one of the captains is a known sports jock. This will increase the likelihood that that person will choose a team of mostly athletes. Give the team of athletes the mushbat, and give the racket to the other team.

Use regular baseball rules—three outs, foul balls, and force-outs. The only thing that differs in this game is that the athletes must hit the ball with the mushbat, and then run around the bases backwards. You could also let only the nonathletic team members use baseball or softball mitts during the game.

After the game is finished, lead a discussion or Bible study on humility, putting yourself in another person's shoes, or empathy. *Dion Reed*

ROUND-THE-BLOCK FRISBEE

Have you ever heard of an evangelistic game of Frisbee? Form two or more teams of youth to play a game of Frisbee in neighborhoods near your church. Be sure to pick areas without heavy traffic or other safety concerns. Each team plays around a different block, and teams should spread out all the way around their assigned areas.

The first player throws the Frisbee to the next person up the street. It's the thrower's responsibility to get the Frisbee to the catcher. If the first throw doesn't make it, the thrower must retrieve the Frisbee and try again. The catcher cannot move. When the catcher successfully catches the Frisbee, then that person becomes the thrower and passes the Frisbee on to the next person. And on it goes around the whole block.

The first team to complete the loop wins. When kids in the neighborhood notice the students playing Frisbee, it's likely they'll come out to join you. Relationships may form and your teenagers can take the opportunity to invite them to attend your youth group or church. *Dan Monnich*

TENNIS TREE

Waiting at camp for your bus to arrive? You can entertain a lot of junior highers outdoors and on the spur of the moment with just a tennis ball and a tree with lots of branches.

Throw the tennis ball as high as you can into the tree. On the way down, it will bounce all sorts of directions before it falls out. All players, including the thrower, have an opportunity to catch the falling tennis ball. Whoever retrieves the ball is the next one to throw it back up into the tree for another round.

Ten points are awarded to the catcher of a no-bouncer. If the ball bounces once, the catcher gets five points. If it bounces twice, the player who catches it gets two points. And if the ball bounces three or more times, the catcher gets zero points. The first player to score 50 points wins.

If the scoring method in the baseball game "500" is familiar to your group, use that system instead: no-bouncer = 100 points, 1-bouncer = 75 points, 2-bouncer = 50 points, 3-or-more bouncer = 25 points. If a player drops or fumbles any of the above catches, he loses the same number of points, going "into the hole" or having a negative score, if necessary. First player to 500 points wins. *Rick Mumford*

TUBE SOCCER

Stack three inner tubes on top of each other and tie them together. Rig some shoulder straps out of rope so each player can wear a stack of tubes. Mark off a rectangular field as you would for a game of regular soccer, with boundary lines, a center line, and a goal at each end.

Divide the kids into two teams of six or more, depending on how many stacks of tubes you create, and play a regular game of soccer. *Nancy Hall*

GLADIATOR RUGBY

Set up your gladiator games course like the diagram below. Tie a piece of string to each of three cloth flags and then attach each one about halfway up a volleyball standard or some other kind of pole.

Choose two student gladiators, and give them matching T-shirts to wear and identify themselves as the gladiators. The total number of contestants is up

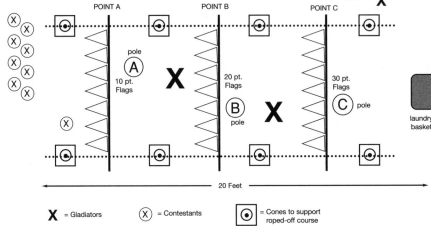

to you. But have a number of adult or student spotters ready to referee the action.

To play, one contestant stands at the starting line (see diagram) with the ball (a football or another ball of similar size). At your signal, she attempts to run to the end of the course and place the ball in the laundry basket inside the goal area to score a point. While a player is running the course, she may choose to go for extra points by grabbing a flag off one of the three poles (see points A, B, or C on the diagram).

Meanwhile, each gladiator has a large pillow in

each hand and uses the pillows to try to push the runner either off the course or down on the ground. A player is considered down if even one knee touches the ground. If the contestant is downed during play, all of her points are lost. Reset the course after each runner's turn.

As time permits, let students run the course more than once and rotate different students in to play the gladiator positions. The student with the most points at the end is the winner. *Rich Griffith*

SHOE LAWN DARTS

Place a hula hoop or a length of rope laid out in a circle about 15 feet away from your players. Ask the kids to line up single file and take off their shoes. The player at the front of the line turns his back to the hoop and tosses his shoes backward over his head—one at a time—toward the hoop. If you're using a rope instead, you can either increase or decrease the diameter of the circle between rounds to change the level of difficulty.

The scoring is simple: five points for any shoe that lands all the way inside the hoop and isn't touching the ring, three points for a shoe that lands on the hoop, and one point if the shoe lands a tube sock's length away from the hoop. The shoe hurler with the most points wins. *Ken Lane*

YOU BRING IT...WE'LL FLING IT!

Set up your playing field with a "fling line" (numbers along a line to represent the teams that will be playing). Add some graduated lines 10 to 300 feet away from the fling line. Draw two bull's-eye targets on either side of the 100-foot line to give your flingers a chance to score even more points for accuracy (see diagram).

See **Build-It-Yourself Balloon Launchers** on page 123 to learn how to make the "funnelator" you need for this activity.

Tell your students in advance that they should each bring something smaller than a bowling ball and they'll get a chance to fling what they bring. When the students arrive, divide them into even teams and have them place their flingable objects on

the fling line next to their teams' numbers.

Before you begin, announce the following award-winning categories: longest flight, most accurate (hits the target), most creative item, messiest fling result, and most points. This last category is determined either by the number of feet divided by 10 or the number hit on the target.

Now tell them the rules. Players should alternate who acts as the holders and the flingers on their team. Students should fire only when instructed to

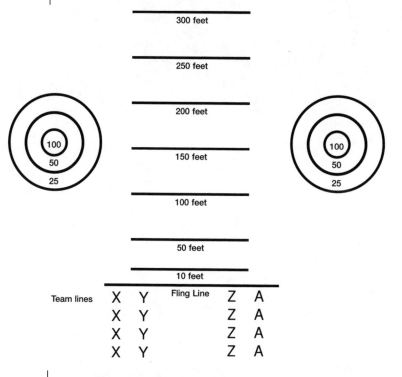

do so by an adult leader. If a flinger misfires, she may re-fling, as long as her item is still intact. Any shots intentionally aimed at anything (or anyone) other than the target area earn an immediate trip home.

You can wrap up a spring or summer fling by giving the students water balloons to fling at the leaders. *Allen Pickett*

RACES AND RELAYS

Nothing fosters a sense of teamwork, camaraderie, and often pandemonium quite like a good old relay race. Relays require team members to perform a given task, one teammate after another, as quickly as possible. Relays call for teams of equal numbers and can be run indoors or outdoors with nearly any size group.

LUCKY CHARMS RACE

Maybe the kids in your group have developed a habit of eating just the marshmallow shapes from their bowls of Lucky Charms. If so, put their skills to the test with this race. The object of the game is to separate the contents of a box of cereal by shape and put the marshmallows into the proper shoeboxes at the other end of the room.

Line up the relay teams on one side of the room. On the other side, spread out eight shoeboxes, one for each shape: pink hearts, yellow moons, orange stars, green clovers, blue diamonds, purple horseshoes, pots of gold, and red balloons. Provide each team with a box of Lucky Charms cereal and have teams choose a runner for each shape. Runners may run down to the shoeboxes only when they have at least 20 pieces in their hands. Meanwhile, the rest of the team members separate the pieces of cereal for the runners.

Give 10,000 points to the team that finishes first. Award 8,500 points for second, 7,500 points for third, and 6,000 points for fourth. After the game, hand out bowls and spoons and provide milk for the kids so the cereal won't go to waste. *Dale Hardy*

BREAD BALL

Have the students split up into even relay teams, with five to 10 players per team. Have the groups line up and give each player a slice of white bread.

When the game starts, the first person on each team pulls the crust off his piece of bread and eats it. Then he takes the crust-less slice, wads it up into a ball, and passes it to the next player in line.

Player two removes the crust from her piece of bread, eats the crust, and then wads up the remaining slice so she can add it to the ball of bread before passing it on to the next person. This continues until the bread ball reaches the last player in line, who must eat not only the crust from his slice of bread, but also the entire bread ball! The first team to finish wins. *Kraig Busman*

PASS THE GRAPES, PLEASE!

This is the old Lifesaver-on-a-toothpick relay race, but with more potential for embarrassment. This isn't a game for particularly conservative churches, but it's a dynamic crowd-breaker for an unchurched kids' outreach event.

All you need are five grapes per coed team of four to 10 kids. Have each team line up single file and stand boy-girl-boy-girl. To start, give each group five grapes and tell players they must use only their teeth to pass each grape to the end of the line. The last person should then eat the grapes. The first team to pass and eat their grapes wins. *Karla Kahler*

RACE FOR THE SUGAR HIGH

For every trio of students you need a small, snack-size bag of chips; a gooey candy bar (like Snickers); and an ice-cold can of soda (Coca-Cola is a good choice because it's so carbonated). Divide your teenagers into threesomes and have the players in each group spread out across the length of the room. Two people should stand near the wall on opposite ends of the room and the third person should be positioned halfway between them. Give the first player in each group a bag of chips, the second a candy bar, and the third a can of soda.

When the signal is given, the players with the chips open their bags and eat all the chips as fast as they can. Then they run and tag the next players on their teams. The second players quickly unwrap and eat the candy bars before they run and tag the third kids. Finally, the last players open and guzzle their cans of soda. The first team to finish wins. If you like, award the winning threesome gift certificates to 7-11 or another convenience store. *Rob Faught*

BAD-BREATH-BUSTER RELAY

Set up your relay teams at one end of the room and adult leaders (one per relay team) at the other. Give each adult a squirt gun and a bottle of mouthwash. The players will sprint down to their team's leader and open their mouths, letting the adult squirt in as much mouthwash as the player can hold. Players then run back to their teams and spit the mouthwash into a large cup. The first team to fill their cup wins. *Paul Johnson*

SOCK HOP

Put two laundry baskets in the middle of the room. Have everyone take off shoes and socks and put one sock into each basket. Mix up the socks thoroughly.

Divide the group into four equal relay teams and have them stand single file, one in each corner of the room.

The players will hop on both feet to the baskets, find both of their socks, put them back on, and then hop back to tag the next people to go. (Note: If you have slick floors, you may want to change the return move to a crabwalk to avoid injuries from slipping and sliding.) The first team to retrieve their socks wins. *Dale Hardy*

TIE MY SHOES

If you don't mind the smell of sweaty feet, here's another game where the only props you need are your students' shoes. Form two relay teams and have players remove their shoes. The right shoes should go in one pile, the left in a separate pile. So each team should have two piles of team members' shoes in front of them—one pile of rights, one pile of lefts.

The first player on each team races to the shoe piles, finds a pair that matches, and ties the laces together—bow-tied, not knotted. (If there are sandals, loafers, or other kinds of shoes without laces in the mix, players should devise some way to link those pairs.) The matched shoes should be dropped into a third pile before the player returns to the team and tags the next runner.

When all the shoes have been matched and linked, the players race again. This time each person chooses a pair of shoes (not her own) and then runs back to her team and gives them to the person they belong to. That player must put on his shoes in a hurry because he's the next runner to go to the shoe pile. The first team to get their shoes back on their feet wins. *Ken Lane*

STINKY FEET GAME

Divide the students into two teams and then split the groups in half again. Half the students on each team should lie on their backs side by side in a line. The rest must each choose one of the prone players as a partner and stand at that person's feet. These players will be doing all the work.

On "go" those who are standing upright take off their partners' shoes. Once all the shoes have been removed, the kids pass a can of air freshener down the line, stopping briefly to spray their partners' bare feet before putting their shoes back on for them. As soon as a player's shoes are on, that person should stand up. The first team to have all their players standing wins. *Ken Lane*

CONCRETE-SHOES RELAY

To vary your next relay, all you need are three boxes of similar size for every pair of players. Teams pair off in line, with partners standing side by side. Each player puts her outside foot in a box and her inside foot in the same box as her partner. So two players share a box between them. Run your relays as you would with individual players, but now each pair must work together to complete the course.

Larger groupings of three, four, or even five students from the same team could also run relays this way. In these cases, the middle people would share both their boxes with the players on either side of them.

Three players would use four boxes, four would use five, and so on. *Len Cuthbert*

ATTACK OF THE CONEHEAD

Designate two points in your youth room that are a good distance apart. One will be the starting point and the other the finish line. Now designate a throwers' area 20 or more feet to the left or right of the path between the two lines (see diagram).

Divide the group into two or more teams. In relay style, a player from each team races from the starting point to the finish line while balancing a small plastic or cardboard cone on his head. He can't touch the cone but also can't let it slide off. If a cone should fall, that player returns to the starting point and begins again.

Meanwhile, the players' teammates gather in the thrower's area and throw Nerf balls at their oppo-

nents to try to knock off the cones as they race by. One person from each team should help retrieve the balls and return them to the throwers.

Once a player reaches the finish line, the next person in line should be ready to pop a cone on her

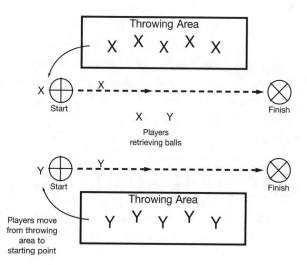

head and go. The first team to get all its players across the finish line wins. *Len Cuthbert*

DISK-TOSS RELAY

So the church finally replaced your old Apple IIe, but your new hard drive won't accept floppy disks? This game will give new life to that old box of diskettes gathering dust on your shelf.

Form two relay teams and line them up eight to 10 feet away from a starting line. Ten to 15 feet away from that, but about a foot in front of a wall or door (which will serve as a kind of backboard), place a bucket for each team. Put a stack of old floppy disks on the starting line, one pile for each team to toss.

When you give the signal, the first player in

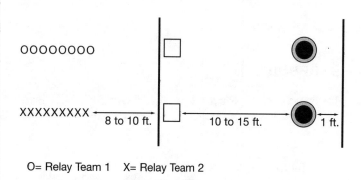

109

each line runs to the starting line, picks up a disk, and tosses it toward the team's bucket. Have a runner retrieve the disks that miss and return them to the thrower. If the disk goes into the bucket directly, that team gets 10 points. If the disk goes into the bucket after hitting the wall or door, that team gets five points. Ask another person to serve as scorekeeper.

Set a time limit for the game, or limit the number of attempts per student. Then give a prize to whoever scores the most points. In case of a tie, have a toss-off overtime period where the most points scored in two minutes wins. *Robin Nakamura*

PADDLE, PADDLE, BASKET

Create relay teams, and give each team three paddles—ping-pong paddles, tennis rackets, or homemade paddles made from clothes hangers and pantyhose. (See **Pantyhose Paddle** on page 56.) Each team also needs several soft six- to eight-inch balls, at least one for every three players on a team, and a large trashcan placed about 20 feet away from where the relay teams line up.

Three players from a team run the relay together. Two members of each triad take paddles and spread out along the path between their teammates and their trashcan, with the third person standing about five feet away from the can.

To start, player one tosses the ball to player two. The second player uses his paddle to bounce the ball to player three, who then paddles the ball into the

goal or trashcan. Whether they make the shot or miss, the three return to their team and hand over their paddles to the next trio of players. Balls that don't land in the goal may be picked up and returned to that team for another set of players to use.

You can score the game in two ways: the team with the most balls in their trashcan after their team finishes wins, or the team with the most balls in their trashcan after 60 seconds wins. *Ken Lane*

CLOTHESPIN RELAY

The kids should line up in teams of five or six. (If your group is small, you can also form one line and play this game non-competitively.) Place a basket, box, or bag of spring-action clothespins (one or two per player) at the front of each team's line. The first player in each line picks up a clothespin and clips it onto the next person. Player two then unclips it and re-clips it to the next person, and so forth on down the line. Players can't hand the clothespins to each other; they must pass them by clipping them onto their teammates' clothing. The last kid in line will eventually receive all the clothespins until the trick becomes finding an empty spot to attach more clothespins.

End the game when either one team has clipped every pin in their bag onto the last kid in line or time has run out. Then count the number of clothespins attached to the last kid in each line to determine the winner.

If you're playing with one line of kids, play for 60 seconds and when time is up, count the number of clothespins the last kid is wearing. Now remove them, rearrange the order of the players, and play for another minute. Compare the number of clothespins that were clipped during the allotted time for each round you play.

Or you could just play until the clothespins run out, and time them to see how long it takes the kids to use them all. Then rearrange the group and have them play again in an effort to beat their last time.
Keith Curran

	20 ft.			
OOOOOOOO	O	O	O ← 5 ft. →	⬤
XXXXXXXX	X	X	X	⬤
AAAAAAAA	A	A	A	⬤
BBBBBBBB	B	B	B	⬤
Teams wait behind this line	Player 1 w/ ball	Player 2 w/ paddle	Player 3 w/ paddle	

O = Team 1   X = Team 2

A = Team 3   B = Team 4

⬤ = Large Trash Can

Izzy-Dizzy Clothespin Relay

String a clothesline across one end of your youth group room and stretch it tight. You can also use a rope or twine, as long as it's taut. Attach some spring-action clothespins to the line, one for every player. You'll also need one baseball bat per team. Halfway between the starting line and the clothesline, lay the bats down in a line with a few feet of space between them (see diagram). This will prevent the dizzy players from running into each other.

Divide the group into even teams and have them line up single file behind the starting line.

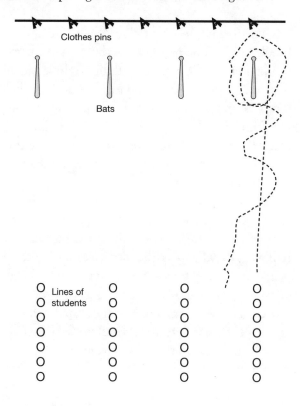

When you say, "Go!" the first players run to their baseball bats and stand them up on end. Bending over at the waist, they place their foreheads on the handles and turn in a circle six, seven, or whatever number of times you say they should spin.

After they've completed their circles, players drop the bats and stagger to the nearby clothesline, where each person retrieves a clothespin with her teeth. Players then run back to their teams to tag the next runners in line. The first team to finish wins. It's hilarious to watch dizzy students try to pick clothespins off the line with their mouths! *Jayson Turner*

Clothespin Chaos Night

To divide your group into teams, number some spring-action clothespins according to how many kids you expect to attend. So if you're expecting 32 kids, write numbers one through 32 on 32 clothespins. Place the clothespins in a box or bowl so when

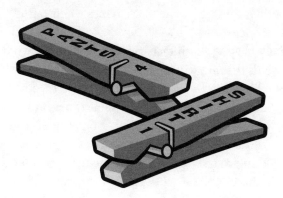

kids arrive, each one can grab a clothespin and find his teammates. (Post a list that states which numbers are on the same team so you don't have to answer that question a hundred times before the meeting gets started!) If you want to have four relay teams, the kids with numbers one through eight, nine through 16, 17 through 24, and 25 through 32 will join to form teams. The following games are not variations on a single game, but a collection of games based on a theme—clothespins.

For the **Body Clipping** game described below, you should also alternate writing the following words or phrases on the numbered clothespins: shirtsleeve, shirttail, shirt collar, pant leg—at the knee, pant cuff, shoe, hair, ear, and finger (see sample picture).
- **Clothes-Liner.** Once they've been assigned to their teams, send the kids to a clothesline (held by two adult leaders), where they should clip their clothespins anywhere on the line. And tell them they need to remember their numbers.

After the relay teams line up, the first person in each line runs to the clothesline to find his numbered clothespin, grabs it with his mouth, and then runs back to tag the next in line. To add some excitement, occasional wiggling of the clothesline by the adults makes the game more difficult and hilarious. The first team to retrieve all their clothespins wins.

• **Licorice Lunch.** Kids remain in their relay teams but with their clothespins in their mouths to start. The first person in each line clips her clothespin onto a licorice twist and passes it to the next person without using her hands. If the licorice is dropped, the person who dropped it must pick it up with the clothespin clenched between his teeth. To win the relay, the last person in line must clip the licorice and then eat it. It's okay to use hands when eating the licorice.

• **Body Clipping.** Each teenager should note the word or words that are written on her clothespin before this relay. With the clothespin between her teeth, the first person clips hers onto the next person in line wherever the clothespin says—on a shirtsleeve or a pant leg, for example. The last person in line should run to the first person on the team in order to clip his clothespin in the proper location and finish the game.

• **Candy Clip and Run.** Throw a handful of wrapped gum and candy into a pile in the center of the room. At the signal, the first person in line runs to the pile with her clothespin between her teeth. Without using her hands, she must retrieve a piece of candy and run back to tag the next person in line. The first team to finish eating their candy wins.

• **Clothespin Closer.** Have the teenagers hang onto their clothespins after the relays are finished. Throughout the night you can randomly draw numbers for some simple giveaway prizes. If a student's number is called, he claims his prize by showing his clothespin. *Dan Doebel*

T-Shirt Relay

Create two equal piles of 10 to 20 large or extra-large T-shirts, one pile for each team. The first person in line takes a shirt, puts it on, and then takes it off again as fast as possible before passing it on to the next player, who does the same. Meanwhile, the first player takes the next shirt from the pile and does it all over again.

As the last person in line removes T-shirts, she should fold them up nicely and make a new stack on the floor next to her. The first team to wear all the T-shirts and put them back in a stack wins. *Ken Lane*

Fashion-Show Race

If you've ever been involved in a theatrical production, you know all about quick costume changes backstage. Here's a relay race that uses this same idea.

Place some old dress-up clothes—a dress, high-heel shoes, a dress shirt, a sport coat, a pair of men's pants, a belt, a tie, a pair of socks, and men's dress shoes—in a box for each team to use, then put the boxes at the opposite end of the room. Divide the group into equal relay teams of at least eight students. Four players from each team will race at one time.

The first four people in line for each team should choose one person to be the dress-up dummy for their group. This player will run to the costume box and put on the dress and high heels. Then he'll run back and get the rest of the mini-team, or the next three people in line. When the four players reach the box, the three work together to take the dress and high heels off of the dummy and then dress him in the man's suit.

Once the suit is on, all four run back to the team and the three dressers work together again to take *off* the suit. When everything has been removed, they hand all the men's clothes to the next person in line, who must run to the other end and put on the dress and high heels, repeating the process all over again. The first dress-up dummy to get rid of the suit, return all the clothes to the costume box, and then run back to stand with her teammates, wins. *John Cosper*

Find-a-Date Relay

Come December, you can buy some old desktop, page-a-day calendars at a great discount for this game. Remove the calendar pages from all the calendars, but keep the pages from each calendar together.

Create as many teams as you have sets of calendar pages, and have them line up single file at one end of the room. At the other end, mix up the pages from each calendar and place them in a messy pile, one per team. Beforehand you should create a list of days the players will need to find. For example, three days in June, any Sunday, one day in March and two days in February, one day from each month, two Mondays and three days in May, four national holidays, and so on.

To begin, tell the first runners what calendar dates they'll be looking for and then give them the signal to go. Runners should bring the correct calendar pages to you or another adult volunteer for verification before returning to their teams. When they do, give them the next days on the list so they can tell their teammates what to look for when they run back and tag them for their turn to go. The first team to correctly find pages for all the days you requested wins. *Ken Lane*

SHREDDED WHEAT

Collect a large amount of shredded paper from some local businesses. Now write out some Bible verses on plain white paper and make as many copies of those sheets as you have teams. Cut the sheets of Scripture into long strips (make them a little wider than the shredded paper ribbons). Make sure you keep a master copy of the passages so you can correctly assess each group's answers at the end of their search.

Divide the paper as best you can into equal piles, one per team of four to six students, and mix the verses into each paper pile. On your signal, the teams race each other to see who'll be the first to find and correctly piece together the buried Bible verses.

This game is a great one to use before a lesson about searching for God's Word—or use it to introduce the Bible passage you plan to teach or speak about that day. *Kraig Busman*

ACTIONARY RELAY

Two equal teams of players line up side by side across the room, but stand facing in opposite directions. An adult leader should stand at one end of each line during the game. The first kids in both lines (in other words, the players who are standing the farthest distance from the adult leaders) are given the same simple word to act out for their teams. However, first they have to run a lap around their teammates. Players should use all the rules of regular Charades.

After a team guesses the word or phrase correct-

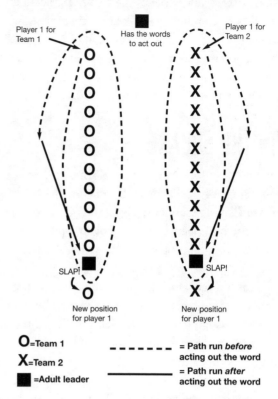

Player 1 for Team 1

Has the words to act out

Player 1 for Team 2

SLAP! SLAP!

New position for player 1 New position for player 1

O=Team 1
X=Team 2
■=Adult leader

- - - - - = Path run *before* acting out the word

———— = Path run *after* acting out the word

ly, the one who acted it out now runs to the leader and slaps her hand. The first team to slap its leader's hand—*not* the first team to guess the word—wins the round. When a player finishes his turn, he should line up on the other side of the adult leader and remain there for the rest of the game.

Now the second player for each team receives a word to act out after running a lap. It continues like this until a team's last player slaps the leader's hand to end the game. The team that finishes with the most first slaps wins. *Mark Lynch and Mark Skoretz*

PLACE YOUR ORDER HERE

For this relay, borrow some Duplo or Lego sets for toddlers. You'll need at least eight blocks for each relay team. On three-by-five cards, write a list of the block colors in different patterns, such as red/yellow/green/green/red/blue/yellow/blue. Make sure you have the same number of card sets with identical block patterns as you have teams.

Give the first player on each team an index card (with the same block order written on it for each team). These players must run to where the Duplo or Lego sets are sitting on tables at the other end of the room and put their blocks together in the right order. After a judge checks their work for accuracy, they should completely break apart their creations, run back to their teams, and tag the next players. The second runner from each team gets a new card that describes a different block arrangement. The first team to fill their orders wins. *Ken Lane*

PIN THE SQUARE

Lay out a four-foot by four-foot playing grid with masking tape (see diagram). Photocopy the **Pin-the-Square Playing Cards** on page 115 and cut them apart. You also need 10 plastic bowling pins or two-liter soda bottles, capped and filled halfway with water.

This is a relay race for two teams. Divide the symbol cards and give half to each team, along with five pins. Assign one adult leader to assist each team during the game by holding and shuffling the symbol cards when necessary.

The teams should line up single file about 10 feet away from the grid on the floor. The first player for each team randomly draws a card and runs to set a bowling pin in that square on the grid. The pin must be standing securely before the player runs back to her team to draw another card and place a pin in the square indicated by the card. Each first

H	3	G	◆	J	O
A	T	✓	4	✳	B
#	8	Z	X	Q	5
1	☆	▲	✝	7	U

player will repeat this process five times during a turn.

Before the second player's turn begins, the adult leader should quickly shuffle the five cards that were drawn by player one. Now player two draws a card from that stack of five, runs to the grid, and retrieves a pin from that space. The second player does this

four more times before it's player three's turn to go.

Now the adult leader shuffles *all* the cards together again and offers player three all 12 cards to choose from. Just as the first player did, now player three will draw five cards—one at a time—and position the pins back on the grid. Then player four will retrieve the pins during his turn. The game ends when all of a team's players have taken a turn and all the pins have been retrieved from the grid. *Rod Nielsen*

FAT THIGHS RELAY

You need four to six small balloons per player and a couple of rolls of masking tape to liven up relay races for your youth group. Just tape inflated balloons to the insides of players' legs so they have to run the race bowlegged to avoid popping the balloons. The winners are those who cross the finish line with the fewest broken or lost balloons. *Len Cuthbert*

LOCKER RELAY

Before your students return to school in the fall or after a holiday break, try this game to get them back into the swing of things. Create some cardboard lockers and spray-paint them different colors. You can use any size cardboard boxes. Just cut each box so the side will open to the right like a door. Poke a hole in the part that swings open and in the left wall of the box. Loop some rope through both holes and tie it into a loop. Now put a combination padlock through the two loops to keep the locker door closed.

Before the game, place inside each locker as many items as there are people on a team. Some suggested items are a brown paper lunch bag stuffed with newspaper and stapled shut, a coat, a shoe, a pencil, a bottle of glue, an apple, a cup, a sock, toilet paper, a notebook, a textbook or a dictionary, notebook paper, an inflated balloon, a roll of tape, a cheerleader's pom-pom, and some scissors. Close the door, attach the combination padlock, and write the combination for the lock on the outside of each locker.

Divide the group into teams, one team per locker full of goodies. At the signal, the first player on each team will run to the locker, unlock the pad-

PIN-THE-SQUARE PLAYING CARDS

Copy this page onto a sheet of card-stock paper and cut the squares apart to make a deck of cards.

lock, retrieve one item from the locker, and then lock it back up before running back to the team. The first player tags the next person in line by handing him the item just retrieved from the locker.

Player two then carries that item with him as he repeats the process. This continues until all the items are out of the locker. It's hilarious to watch players juggle 12 or more items while trying to open the padlock and get one more. The first team to successfully remove everything from their locker wins.

Susan Grapengater

TABLE-CLOCK RELAY

Use masking tape to divide a rectangular table into six to eight equal sections (see diagram). Do this to as many tables as you have teams, then line up the tables at one end of the room. Place a large plastic cup on each table. Form your teams and give each player a small, deflated balloon. Have players line up on the other side of the room from their tables.

The first runner on each team races to the team's table, bends over the cup so part of her balloon is inside the cup, and blows up her balloon just enough so she can pick up the cup using only the inflated balloon to hold it. If the cup falls—even if it falls on the floor—a player is not allowed to touch it with her hands. She must use the balloon to pick it up again. Once she's able to pick up the cup, she

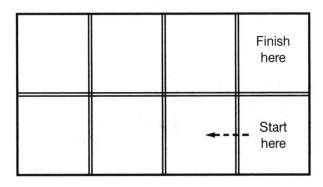

			Finish here
			← - - - Start here

should move it to the next square on the table, run back to tag the next player, and return to the end of the line. After three minutes, the team that advanced its cup the farthest wins. *Ken Lane*

MAMA BIRD

First you need to assemble two mama-bird facemasks (see illustration). Poke a golf tee out through the bottom of a Styrofoam cup. Tie a rubber band on each side of the cup, close to the rim. Loop another rubber band around the two that are attached to the cup so you have loops to go around the player's ears. Place another cup inside the first to help hold the golf tee in place.

At one end of the room, set up a table with two paper plates full of jumbo-size marshmallows, one marshmallow per team member. Split the kids into two teams of baby birds, and have them line up on the other side of the room from the table of marsh-

mallows. Each team should choose a player to be the mama bird. Give each mama bird a facemask to wear.

At your signal, each mama bird runs to his team's plate of marshmallows, pokes his golf-tee beak into one marshmallow, and takes it back to feed one of his baby birds. Then he goes back for another marshmallow. The babies have to use their mouths to remove and eat the marshmallows—no hands allowed! The first mama bird to feed all his babies is the winner.

A variation of this game is to have the mama bird feed the first baby, then give that player the mama bird mask to put on and have that person go get a marshmallow in order to feed the next baby bird in line. Meanwhile, the first mama bird goes to the end of the line and becomes a baby bird. Keep rotating until the first mama bird is at the front of the line again. *CAC*

TIL SOMEONE LOSES AN EYE

It's all fun and games until… Your junior highers will love this game. Not only do they get to throw things, but they get to aim for their leaders' faces!

For each team, tape a Styrofoam plate to the bill of a baseball cap. When the bill of the cap is flipped up, the Styrofoam plate should hang down right in front of the wearer's face. For added effect, you can draw a bull's-eye on each plate or even write some taunting words. Ask each of your adult leaders to put on a hat and stand at one end of the room.

Now divide the students into as many teams as you have leaders wearing hats, and have students line up single file at the other end of the room. About 10 feet in front of the leaders, create your ammunition station. You can stock it with stacks of scrap paper, loaded squirt guns, bottles of squeezable mustard or ketchup (have the leaders stand on plastic if you use condiments for your ammo), Nerf balls, and other harmless objects.

When you give the signal, the first player on each team runs to the supply station, grabs some ammo, and aims for the plate of that team's adult leader. If she's hit, the leader should make some sort of noise to indicate that the player hit the target, and then the player returns to the end of his team's line so the next player can go. Leaders should try to keep track of how many hits are made against their plates. After the first team finishes, the hits are counted and the one with the most direct hits wins. *Brad Sorensen and Ben Nesdoly*

EMPTY THAT BOX

You need a small box of pop-up tissues for each team. Open the boxes ahead of time so the first tissue is sticking out of the top of each box. Each player will race to her team's box of tissue and—with her hands behind her back—pull out a tissue with her mouth. When she has a tissue between her teeth, she runs back to her team and tags the next runner before depositing the tissue in a waste-basket at the end of the line. This continues until a team completely empties their box. *Ken Lane*

THE GREAT TISSUE BLOW

This dizzying game is fun to watch. Form relay teams and give each player a tissue. Make a line about 20 feet away from where the relay teams are lined up. To begin the relay, the first players blow their tissues into the air and *keep* blowing as they walk toward the finish line. A tissue cannot be touched or allowed to fall to the floor, or the player must go back and start again. As soon as a player successfully reaches the finish line, the next player on the team blows. The team to get all their tissues across the line first wins. *Ken Lane*

TOILET PAPER BLOW OUT

Can you spare a square? Divide your group into two teams. Line up the teams at opposite ends of the room, and place a square of toilet paper on the floor in the middle of the room. Have each team stand at one end of the room. Mark a goal line about four feet in front of where each team is standing. This will keep players from interfering while they're waiting for their turn to play.

The object of the game is to get the square of TP across the opposing team's goal line by blowing it. A player from each team will face off in the middle, but each gets just two blows before running back and tagging the next person on the team. The team with the most hot air will undoubtedly win this one. *Ken Lane*

PLUMBER MOVER

Set up a simple obstacle course in a room with a tiled floor or another smooth surface. Each player needs something to kneel on that's large enough to sit on and has wheels on the bottom—a furniture mover, a skateboard, those things mechanics use to slide underneath cars, whatever you can find.

Once a player is situated on her wheeled "ride," give her two clean plungers. She'll use these to propel herself forward by pushing the plungers down onto the floor, pulling herself forward, and then releasing the plungers so she can do it all over again.

Hint: Players should choke up on the plungers and pull hard! They're very hard to control.

Players will race against the clock as they maneuver through the obstacle course before crossing the finish line on the other side. The player with the best finish time wins. *Ken Lane*

BOTTOM-BALLOON-PLUNGER RELAY

Form relay teams with an even number of students on each team. Every team should pair off before the race begins. Give a plunger to the first two runners from each team. The students should stand back to back, then bend forward at the waist. Each partner should put the rubber part of a plunger between his legs. Now place an inflated balloon between the two plunger handles.

The players walk to the other side of the room in this position, while keeping the balloon from touching the floor. If the balloon drops, the pair must start all over again. Once partners reach the finish line, both players run back and hand their plungers and balloon to the next pair. *Ken Lane*

PAPER SCOOT

So you've got a tower of old newspapers that's out of control?

To start, a player places her feet on opposite corners of a large sheet of newspaper (students should do this race in their socks). In order to move toward the finish line, she must slide her feet together and then move one foot forward in the direction she wants to go. She must be very careful not to tear the newspaper. If it gets torn, the player must return to

the beginning, get a fresh sheet of newspaper, and try again.

Once a player reaches the finish line, the next player in line may go, using his section of the paper. The first team to move their stack of newspapers from one end of the room to the other wins. *Ken Lane*

PINBALL-SHUFFLE RELAY

Line up a group of players in front of a pinball machine, and insert some coins to get the game going. From this point on, the score is irrelevant. The first player standing in front of the machine plays until the first hit is made with a flipper. Then that player moves to the back of the line and the next person moves ahead to control the flippers. At the next hit of the flipper, the front person moves to the back of the line and so on.

If the ball is lost, the player standing at the front of the line when the ball goes down the drain is out of the game. Play until only one person is left. *Gary Sivewright*

WHEELBARROW RELAY

Divide your kids into teams of two to make human wheelbarrows. Set up an empty kiddie pool some distance away from the starting point. The idea is for the wheelbarrow to put some object (your choice) in the pool by carrying it in a spoon in a player's mouth. To spice this up, join several pairs into a team and have them go to the pool and back in some special formation, such as a cross, triangle, or starburst (a form something like an asterisk).

GAMES

Who says you need a pool or lake to enjoy liquid fun? These games are the ticket to refresh your kids on a hot summer day. Whether the games involve water balloons or Super Soakers, your group is guaranteed a sopping good time.

THE GREAT BUBBLE BLOW-OFF

Place bubble soap in some one-gallon buckets, one bucket per team, then fill them halfway with water. Wipe the inside of the top half of each bucket dry with a rag to keep the bubbles from breaking too soon.

Line up the relay teams at the opposite end of the room from the buckets, and give each player a straw. Each runner will run to the team's bucket, place the straw in the water, and start blowing. Each group of players should be allowed only a few seconds of blowing before you signal for them to return to their teams and tag the next players.

The first team to make their bubbles go over the top of the bucket wins. *Ken Lane*

HATCH A WATER BALLOON

Need a relay to cool your kids' jets on a hot summer day? Three or four even teams line up around and equidistant from a kiddie pool filled with water and water balloons. Halfway between the pool and each line of kids, place a plastic lawn chair (the kind with drain slots or holes in the seat) and put a small

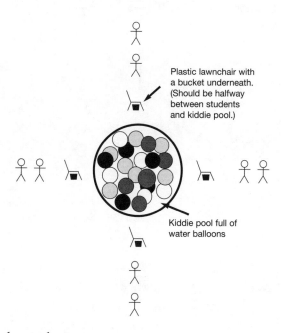

Plastic lawnchair with a bucket underneath. (Should be halfway between students and kiddie pool.)

Kiddie pool full of water balloons

bucket under it.

Each player runs to the pool, picks up a balloon with her mouth, and carries it back—still between her teeth—to the lawn chair. After she places the balloon on the seat of the chair, she must pop the balloon with her own seat. As soon as the balloon pops, the next player can run to the pool. Meanwhile, the water from the broken balloon drains into the bucket below. The first team to fill their bucket wins. *Len Cuthbert*

OPERATION BUCKET BOMB

This relay game will get your kids moving in some brand-new ways. First, drive four sharpened nails or spikes in through a plastic bucket (one for each team) so the pointed ends are facing into the center. Place a brick or a large rock in the bottom of the pail to keep it upright. Fill an equal amount of water balloons for each team (at least one per player). Tie a looped string around the end of each balloon so you can attach the balloon to a bungee cord.

Each runner gets a water balloon attached to his waist using a bungee cord that's hung from his back-center belt loop. The cord should be short enough so it won't drag, but long enough so a player can't squat and burst the balloon. One person per team should act as a "deckhand" to help attach the water balloons to the runners' belt loops. To keep the game moving, the deckhands should have a bucket full of water balloons nearby, and they should work to make sure more

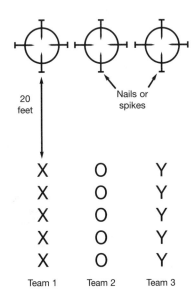

20 feet

Nails or spikes

X O Y
X O Y
X O Y
X O Y
X O Y

Team 1   Team 2   Team 3

than one player is outfitted with a water balloon so players are ready to run when tagged.

Relay teams line up about 20 feet away from their buckets (see diagram). On your signal, the first runner for each team races to the team's pail. If the balloon bursts while the player is running, the player must go back to the deckhand and get a new balloon. When a player finally reaches the bucket, he positions himself over the bucket and—without using his feet, legs, or hands— tries to swing the balloon into the bucket until it bursts on the nails or spikes. He may have to do this over and over in

order to break the balloon. After the balloon is broken, he runs back to his team and tags the next runner. Then he should give his bungee cord to the deckhand so it can be attached to one of his teammates. The first team to fill their bucket with water wins. Sit back and watch some hilarious gyrations! *Ray A. Jones, Jr.*

SPONGES RELAY

Give each relay team two five- or 10-gallon buckets (one bucket color for each team, if possible). One of the buckets should be full of water and placed near the head of the line. The empty bucket should be placed about 15 feet away from the front of the line.

The object of the game is to use a large sponge to move all the water from the full bucket to the empty one in the least amount of time. Entire teams may have to take more than one turn to accomplish this soggy task. Drips are inevitable, so have rolls of paper towels on hand. But if a team spills a quarter of a cup of water or more during the transfer, that team is out. The first team to fill their empty bucket wins. *Josh Conn*

WATER-BOWL RACE

Relay teams run this race in pairs. Give each team a two-by-four piece of wood with a plastic bowl full of water sitting on it. At the two ends of the room, each team should have their own five-gallon buckets, one full of water (for refilling the plastic bowl) and the other one empty.

The first pair of runners on each team stands back-to-back and straddles the two-by-four. The partners should pick it up, being careful not to spill the water, and hold the board between their legs as they walk to the other end of the room. Have someone on hand to help them empty the water into their team's bucket.

The empty bowl is placed back on the wood before the pair hurries back to their team and hands the piece of wood and the bowl to the next pair of players. The bowl must be refilled with water before this new pair can go. Whichever team gets the most water into their bucket during two rounds of play (in other words, after all the players have gone twice) wins. *Ken Lane*

WATER-BAG ATTACK

During this soggy game, teams create their own ammunition to use against their opponents. Two teams stand on opposite ends of the playing area with Ziploc sandwich bags and two large buckets of water (one per team). Two empty buckets, one per team, should be placed at each end of the playing area, and players aren't allowed to get within two feet of them during the game. Create a center line on the playing field.

Players fill their Ziploc bags with water, seal them, and try to hurl them into the opposing team's buckets from behind the center line. They must also defend their own team's buckets. As long as a bag hasn't fallen into the no-enter zone around the goal, it can be picked up and thrown again by either team.

Play as long as energy levels are high and there's still water left in the buckets for refilling the baggies. Then count the number of bags in each bucket. A team earns five points for each baggie in their opponent's buckets. Now empty any baggies that didn't already break open on impact and see how much water is in each bucket. Award another 20 points to the team with the smallest amount of accumulated water in their bucket. *Len Cuthbert*

WATER-BALLOON GOLF

If you live near a Frisbee golf course, it would be an ideal location to play this game; but a park, a pasture, or any wide-open area with trees and few people will work. Play with teams of three, fill about 40 water balloons per nine holes, and place them in backpacks to transport them around the course. Bring along some of those large water-balloon launchers that shoot at least 200 feet. Toys 'R' Us carries them for $10 to $15 each, but any large toy store should have them in stock. (See **Build-It-Yourself Balloon Launchers** if you're interested in making your own launchers.) One launcher per trio of players is more than enough. Everyone could use one launcher during the game without too much trouble.

Players use the balloon launchers to try to break each water balloon in a hole on the course (or on a tree, if you aren't using a Frisbee golf course). If the

BUILD-IT-YOURSELF BALLOON LAUNCHERS

To make inexpensive water-balloon launchers, you need the following materials: five to 10 feet of surgical tubing that's one-half inch in diameter (you can get this from a medical supply company), a funnel with a six-inch-diameter mouth, four one-inch hose clamps, a drill, PVC pipe (optional), and some duct tape.

On opposite sides of the funnel, drill two holes that are 3/8" in diameter and about 1/4"

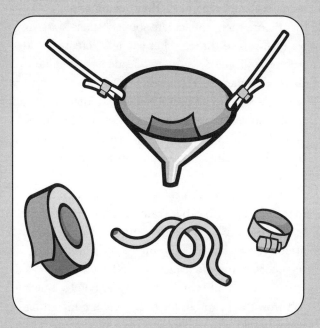

below the rim. Cut the tubing in half and feed three inches of the first length into one hole. Then slip the hose clamp onto both ends of the tube to join them together. Tighten the hose clamp, then repeat this process with the other length of tubing. At the other ends of the tubing, fold over the tubing to make handles, and use the other hose clamps to solidify them, or use pieces of PVC pipe on the ends of the surgical tubing for handles.

Now use some duct tape to make a cradle inside the funnel. Without this part, when the balloon is released, it will squeeze down inside the hole and burst. Pick up any balloon fragments after the game. *Derek Maxson* balloon unintentionally breaks in an overhanging tree, the player must play through from under the spot where it broke. Players go through the whole course. *Barrett Hendrickson*

WATER BOMBS WITH A CHALLENGE

If you have some time to set this up and an hour or two to kill with your students on a warm afternoon, here's a game for at least four teams of six or more players. It's also a good way to teach your students about trust. Each team has a leader and a co-leader who are briefed on the game ahead of time. They, in turn, explain the game to their teammates.

Before the game, create some obstacle stations for teams to go through. For example, create a spider web out of ropes that the two leaders must guide their team members through, or have each player try to kick a soccer ball past a goalie and into a net, and so on. However, players must complete all the obstacles while blindfolded. As teams successfully finish the task at each station, each player receives a water bomb.

As players move from station to station, they may meet up with other teams. At those points the leaders must make a choice—attack or run! The attack can be carried out only by the blindfolded members, while the leaders verbally guide them as to where they should throw their water bombs, how far to throw them, and so forth. If there are incoming water bombs, the two leaders must protect their teammates by shielding them with their own bodies. The winner will be the driest team, but by the end no one will really care who wins. *Kenneth Lam*

ZIGZAG SOAK

There's nothing like a soaking-wet obstacle course to cool off your kids on a hot summer day. The object of this game is for students to run through a zigzag course without getting hit by water-soaked sponges thrown by the opposing team.

To set up the zigzag maze, design seven or more Safe Spots (see diagram) along the path, using bales of hay or straw, cardboard appliance boxes, chairs, ropes, freshman students—whatever! The Safe Spots provide some protection for the runners from their opponents.

Near the end of the course, add a Challenge Box where players must complete some physical challenges before they're done—pushing an earth ball 10 feet, jumping rope 20 times, doing 15 jumping jacks—all while being pelted with wet sponges.

The players running the course are attackers, and it's best if they run in pairs. Attackers must

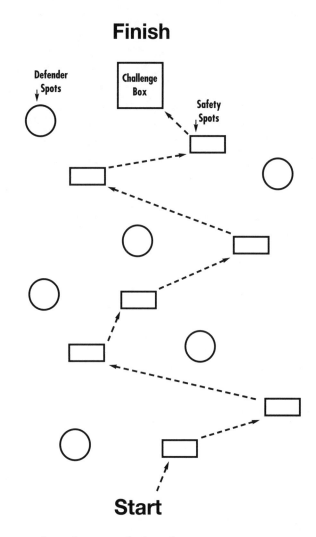

Finish

Defender Spots

Challenge Box

Safety Spots

Start

touch each station before they attempt to move on to the next one. If one of the attackers is hit, she's out and her companion continues the course alone.

The sponge throwers are defenders, and they must stay within their Defender Spots—designated by *you*—between stations. To make sure the defenders stay put, you could have them stand inside hula hoops or mark off their areas in some other obvious way.

Each of these defender spots should have a five-gallon bucket of water and five to seven sponges in her space. Water balloons are a fun vari-

124

ation here. You'll need *lots* of water, and it helps to play this game near a hose. Defenders are allowed to throw their sponges only when an attacker is even with them or past them—not before they reach the defenders' spot. It's wise to point out that if they throw toward the next terminator in front of them, the sponges won't be lost and terminators further up the field will have more sponges to throw at the attackers—or maybe it's more fun *not* to point that out. You may choose to have one fabulous spot near the center of the maze where defenders are allowed to throw sponges in any direction. And give extra sponges to each defender in this location.

Scoring is optional, but if you do score, give one point to the defenders for each attacker they hit with a sponge. Attackers who successfully complete the course and stay dry doing it score five points for their team. However, scores don't really matter. The whole point of the game is to get wet and have fun.

When all the students have played a round as the attackers, send the youth workers through and give the teenagers a shot. Chances are good that those buckets themselves will start flying now! *Rusty Thomas*

ULTIMATE WARRIORS

Set up the same kind of course as the one used in **Zigzag Soak** on page 124. About 20 yards from the beginning of the course, set up some kind of target, such as a trashcan lid, a table turned on its side, a car, folding chairs, whatever. At each of the "safe spots" along the course, the runner should stop and try to hit the target with a tennis ball from behind each barricade. A bucket of balls can be stored at each safe spot for the runners to use. However, each player gets only one throw per safe spot.

Meanwhile, the Ultimate Warriors hurl their supply of water balloons at the contenders who are weaving their way through the course. If a runner is hit with a balloon, that person is out. Time the runners, and award the grand prize to the player with the fastest time and the driest run through the course. *Nathan Cook*

SUPER SOAKER FLOATER

To prepare for this game, fill some Super Soaker water guns and inflate lots of balloons (one per player). Each player tries to stay in the game by squirting a balloon with the water to keep it in the air. No part of a player's body or water gun may touch the balloon, and the balloon obviously can't touch the floor or that player is out. *Len Cuthbert*

CARD SHARKS

When the music starts, a circle of players passes around a toy shark (or any object) until the music stops. The person holding the shark at this point becomes "It," and whoever is sitting directly across the circle from that person gets to hold a fully loaded Super Soaker or another type of water gun.

Now It chooses a playing card from a full deck to determine his fate. If an ace or a face card is drawn, It gets blasted by the Super Soaker. If It chooses a black number card, the person on his left gets the blast of water. And if a red number card is drawn, the person sitting to the right of It is the soggy target.

Whoever got drenched gets to hold the water gun for the next round and waits with great anticipation for a new victim to be chosen by the luck of the draw after the music stops playing. *Stephen C. Deutsch*

DRINK THAT WATER

Fill two bowls with water and give two contestants teaspoons. When the signal is given, the players race to empty their bowls. They do this by drinking the water with their teaspoons. When they get to the bottom of their bowls, they may pour the last of the water into the teaspoon and drink it. The first player to finish wins!

Make this game into a relay by having students race to their bowls, which are sitting on a table at the other end of the room. Have people nearby who are ready to hand out clean spoons and refill the bowls with water between runners. *Ken Lane*

Hidden-Guzzle Relay

Lay a table on its side at the front of the room. Behind it—out of sight of the players—place an odd number of uncapped bottled waters (to avoid a tie). Form two teams, line them up at the other end of the room, and give each player a straw.

The first person from each team runs behind the table and uses her straw to drink from any bottle. When you say stop, she must stop run back to her team to tag the next player. If a player empties the bottle she was drinking from before you yell, "Stop!" she takes it back with her to her team. Once all the bottles have been emptied, the game is over, and the team with the most bottles is declared the winner.

Ken Lane

Dunk, Dunk, Whoosh

Everyone sits in a circle, and the person who is "It" walks around the outside saying, "Dunk, dunk…" while holding a large container full of water. Once It has chosen his victim, he dumps the water on her—that's the whoosh. Then "It" gets chased around the circle by the soaking wet person and sits down in the victim's empty spot. If It is tagged before he can safely sit down, then he must go back to the middle and everyone in the circle gets to dump water on him. *Russell Waddell*

Fish Find

Fill several kiddie pools with water (one pool for each team of 10 or 12 players) and place a bucket half full of water in the middle of each pool. Now put an equal number of minnows in each pool—50 to 75.

Teams sit on their knees around the pools and try to catch the minnows with their hands and transfer them into the buckets in the middle of the pools. The team that moves all their minnows first is the winner.

Now release the minnows back into each kiddie pool and play again—only this time with eyes closed. Then play a third time, again with eyes closed, and add four goldfish to each kiddie pool. This time the kids should try to put the goldfish into the bucket but no minnows. *Bob Anderson*

Jonah's Revenge

Fill two large mixing bowls or buckets (something the kids can fit their heads into) with water and a variety of small live fish. This works best if the water isn't too deep. Two teenagers compete against each other to see who can be the first to put her head in the water and catch a fish in her mouth.

You can give out a range of points for the amount of time it took to catch a fish, the type of fish caught, and so on. No fish need to be harmed, since the kids only catch them with their mouths and then spit them back into the containers. Emphasize the non-cruelty clause of the game! And hand out breath mints or gum after this game! Phew! *Derek Bethay*

Bass, Bass, Bass Basketball

Before you play this game, see if you can find someone to donate a box or more of frozen fish of any kind, the smellier the better—like mackerel. Divide the group into even teams and assign each team a kiddie pool with two or three inches of water in it. Spread out the pools so there's about 10 feet between them. Now place an equal number of almost-thawed fish in each kiddie pool. (If the fish are completely frozen, the fins may cut the kids' skin.)

Have all players remove their shoes and socks. Give the teams a time limit during which they may use only their feet to move the fish to other teams' pools. Teams will need to work fast because their opponents will also be putting fish into their pools.

Assign a point value to each type of fish. When time is up, tally the scores. Play a few rounds and increase the point values each time. *Julia Coon*

Illuminated Water-Balloon Football

Buy an Illuminator Sports Ball or Football (www.funworx.com or 888-388-6559)—they each cost about $13. Fill lots of water balloons and place half of them in a bucket in each end zone. Finally, mark your end zones so they'll glow in the dark, and you're ready to go.

This game is a combination of regular football and Speedball—but outside and after dark. Players may only pass the ball to each other. Otherwise it's too dangerous to play, especially when kids have different levels of athletic skill. So the ball gets tossed along from player to player until a touchdown or turnover occurs.

A tackle is made by soaking a player with a water balloon. Players get the water balloons from their end zones and carefully pass them up and down the field to their teammates until someone on defense can get close enough to soak the player who is holding the ball. (Be careful to keep the ball from getting too wet, or it may stop working.) Teams get the same four downs as in football, but players get soaked each time they're tackled—which is a cooler alternative to using those flag-football belts. *Paul Brown*

Fluid Frisbee Ball

Use three kiddie pools for first, second, and third bases. For the home stretch and home plate, use a Slip 'N Slide with a splash pool at the end of it. Play a game of baseball without a ball, a bat, mitts, or steals. No one pitches, but a player can stand in the traditional pitcher's spot. Hint: It helps to use a catcher.

The batter throws a Frisbee and runs the bases as if she has just hit a fly ball in the World Series. Players get each other out just as in the game of baseball, but as a bonus, they may also hit a runner with the Frisbee to get an out.

To score a run, the runner must slide down the Slip 'N Slide and splash into home plate. Extra points may be awarded for style or subtracted for a lack of it.

To provide variety, fill the wading pools with whipped cream and marshmallows, Jell-O, or even Yuck, which you can purchase through Rec FX Inc. (see **YUCK** on page 86 for more information).

J. Daniel Hutchins

Mongo Cricket

Play this version of cricket on a basketball court. Use a short, fat, plastic children's bat and Nerf ball. For wickets, stack five paper cups as shown in the diagram and fill the top cup with water. Make

three wickets. Have a nearby water supply and keep a mop or some towels handy—you'll get wet with this one!

Set the three wickets on the free-throw line and home plate a foot in front of them. The base is on the basketball court three-point line. The pitcher stands between the base and home plate. No area is out of bounds, even behind the wickets. Players from either team can stand anywhere on the playing field.

The objective of the offense (pitcher's team) is to knock over the wickets. Each wicket knocked over scores a point. The objectives of the defense (batter's team) to protect the wickets and keep them from being knocked over and to score points by running from home plate to the base and back again.

Batters are out if any of the following happens:
- If a hit is caught in the air.
- If tagged while running between home plate and the base by an opposing team player who is holding the ball.
- If an offensive player knocks over a wicket with the ball. The pitcher might knock wickets over during a pitch or other teammates may throw the

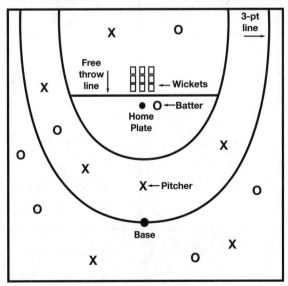

X= offense
O= defense

127

ball at the wickets while the batter is running between bases.

Each team gets three outs. To increase participation use more bases. *Ted Martin*

Ping-Pong Water Polo

Fill a kiddie pool with water and use pieces of duct or electrical tape to mark off two three-inch-wide goal areas on opposite sides of the pool. Teams of two or three gather around the pool on their knees. Each team tries to blow a ping-pong ball into their opponent's goal area for points, at the same time keeping the ball away from their own goal.

Soggy Wads War

Set up your playing field like the diagram below. Place a bucket of water on each side of the playing area, but between the two teams on that side. These buckets are used for re-soaking wads of toilet paper between rounds. Divide the group into four teams.

Each team receives four rolls of toilet paper for ammunition and a trashcan lid with a handle for a shield.

At the beginning of each round, each team sends a gladiator with shield and a soggy wad of toilet paper into the playing arena. At the whistle, the gladiators remain in their own squares, but throw their wads of toilet paper at each other.

If a gladiator is hit in the torso (chest, stomach, back), he's out for that round. A hit on a limb is treated as a strike against the gladiator. If the gladiator is hit a second time on that same limb, she's out. If a gladiator catches a roll of toilet paper in his shield, he can use that wad in addition to his other three rolls.

Each gladiator gets two minutes and three toilet-paper throws. Whoever survives the two-minute onslaught is the winner. Three new players resoak their teams' wads of TP, take up their shields, and enter the arena for their two minutes of glory against the current champion. *Jim Hayne*

Torpedo Ice Cubes

Play this game in a large room with an uncarpeted floor. Have the group sit in a circle around the outside perimeter of the room, and choose one person to be in the middle. The kids should number off going back and forth across the circle (see diagram). These numbers determine the order in which the ice cubes will be shot. The ice cubes will eventually break up, so have a tray or two of replacements on hand.

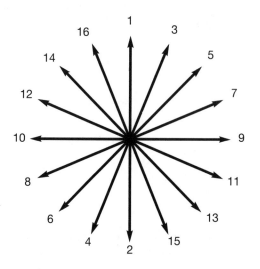

Hand player number one an ice cube. She should shoot it across the floor to player number two, then from two to player three, and so on. Meanwhile, the person in the middle tries to stop the cube, using only his feet. When the cube is stopped, the person who hurled it switches places with the person in the middle. Add extra cubes during the game to create some chaos. *Len Cuthbert*

SLIPPERY WATERMELON

Bring a few watermelons and some jars of Vaseline to your next pool party and try this teamwork game. Divide the group into teams, and have all the kids stand in the pool. Coat the watermelons with Vaseline and throw them in with the students. The object is for one of the teams to be the first to get their watermelon out of the pool. It's much harder than it sounds!

SYNCHRONIZED SWIMMING

Have the kids get into pairs or groups of four outside the pool. Have each group create an entry and routine for the synchronized swimming competition. Give them about five minutes to prepare.

Now, one at a time, each group enters the shallow end of the pool to perform. Play some strange music in the background (try classical or New Age—no Top 40!), and have them do their routine to the music.

Ask a panel of judges to cast their votes for the best routine—and videotape the competition so you can show them how hilarious they looked. *Jada Conrad*

WIDE
GAMES

"Wide games" are games requiring teams to strategize, organize, and assign tasks. They call for more than the usual planning, stealth, and skill. Most wide games—sometimes called adventure games—have a theme, like spies or secret agents, armies at war, and the like. Most require a good deal of space, such as an open field or a wooded area with places to hide.

007

Teens enjoy mysteries, and this challenging 007 adventure will soon be the favorite of your teens. The student teams search for secret agents—who give them clues to the other secret agents—before assassins can, uh, assassinate the agents. The object of the game is to be the first team to figure out all the clues and get back to headquarters.

To begin preparations, contact four area store managers for permission to play the game in their stores. No need to alarm anyone unnecessarily. If playing with squirt guns is a problem, switch to Nerf balls or some other harmless option. Also enlist the help of eight adults—who the kids don't know—to play the agents and assassins.

Prepare passwords—brief conversations that identify the agent and the 007 team to each other. Use Bible verses or odd statements like—

007: For by grace you have been saved.
Agent: Not as a result of works.
007: Never sneeze on a skunk.
Agent: Earthquakes make me itch.

You can make the password several lines long, so each student has a part and to give the assassin more time to ambush the secret agent. You want the kids to be distracted so they are less likely to defend themselves from the assassin and consequently have to do crazy tasks.

Create 5 sets of messages that direct teams from headquarters to each store in sequence and back to headquarters. Each secret agent has a different message from the other agents and will give all the teams the same message. For example the grocery store agent gives each team a message to go Wal-Mart, and the Wal-Mart agent gives each team a message to go to Target, and so on. The messages can be in code (A=B, B=C, etc.) and perhaps also in riddle form.

Supply each assassin with a squirt gun. Each assassin roams around her assigned store, waiting for the 007 team to arrive. The assassins lurk in the background, waiting for kids to locate their secret agent.

Each 007 team needs an adult leader-driver who accompanies the team into the store—and drives the car, of course. All the students need squirt guns, and the team needs a few dollars to buy candy, too.

When the kids arrive at the meeting, the assassins and secret agents should already be on their way to the stores.

Divide kids into four 007 teams. Introduce the game with comments like this—

It's good to have you on the team! Once again the Evil Dark Nation (EDN) threatens the survival of the entire modern world as we know it. To stop this evil force from continuing its tyrannical ravaging of society, you must collect an item from each of our four agent locations in the field. Bring those items back to headquarters as quickly as you can before EDN has a chance to finish its destruction. These four items are absolutely essential to the development of the only defense mechanism against EDN.

Explain the password and the details of the game (still to come…). After the kids are clear on what to do, hand out squirt guns to each player and a clues to different stores to each team. (You don't want two teams at the same store at the same time.) As soon as the teams figure out their first clue, they leave for that location.

When the team gets to the store, they have to figure out who the secret agent is, so they can get their next clue. The team members all stick together. One member of the team says the password phrase to the potential secret agent. If they don't get the right response, they move on. If they do receive the correct response, the secret agent gives the team the clue to the next store.

In the meantime, the assassin is watching. He tries to shoot the agent before the password can be completed and the clue passed to the team. If the assassin is successful, the 007 team has to do a task, such as playing leap frog down the store isle, before they can take the clue from the secret agent's hand. Once an agent is out of the way, the assassin can shoot a team member. If a team member is shot, the team has to buy candy before it can continue. M&Ms, Skittles, and Starbursts divide up well at the end.

The 007 team can defend itself by shooting the assassin before he shoots the secret agent. If the

assassin is shot, he must walk away and wait for the next 007 team to arrive.

For an unexpected ending, just before the team is ready to leave the last store, the driver pulls out a squirt gun and shoots the team, making them buy more candy. The driver tells the 007 team that she is a double agent and hands them an envelope with a note inside. The note gives directions for the team to wait at the front door for a back-up agent to arrive. The double agent drives away—around the block or the parking lot—and returns as the back-up agent to pick up the 007 team right where she left them. The students *never* expect this!

The team that gets through all four stores and back to the church first saves the world from destruction. Their reward is sharing all the candy the rest of the 007 teams bring back to headquarters.

For variety, you can direct kids to other busy public places like a park, skating rink, or beach/lake. If you have a large group, increase the number of teams and locations, or if your time is short, decrease the number of locations. You can have more locations than teams if you think a new group might arrive before the last one has left. *Stephen Evitt*

CLUE DUNNIT?

This game is played in five rooms. You need at least 11 actors—preferably adults who can stay in character. There are five suspects in the murder; five secret agents; one detective; and additional optional roles of deputies, photographers, and protected witnesses. Give them all funny costumes to wear, and the suspects should have silly names like Matt Metaphor, Eileen Erroneous, and so on. The character names will give these actors some insight into how they should act during the game. This game lasts between 45 and 60 minutes when played with a group of 40 to 70 people. Take a Polaroid picture before the game that depicts the murder in the chosen room with the chosen weapon, suspect, and victim.

The game begins subtly, unannounced to the students, with the appearance of the five suspects in costume. Shortly after, the detective appears (perhaps accompanied by deputies) and begins walking around and asking students if they've seen any shady characters around lately. It's up to the detective to promote the game through her questions and how she plays up the role. She begins by announcing that there has been a murder and that she, the detective, is searching for suspects.

After several minutes of questioning, the detective gathers the students and officially asks them to assist her in discovering the murderer. (She could hand out deputy badges to the students at this time, if you like.) Now the detective introduces the suspects to the students, describing them, their habits, past offenses, and other pertinent information. The suspects must also play up their assumed characters in order to create anticipation for the kids. Then the five secret agents, having interspersed themselves throughout the group of kids, are called out of hiding and introduced to the students. Again, to promote excitement, give each an area of expertise in one of the five crime categories: suspect, victim, weapon, room, and motive.

At this point, the suspects head off to their designated rooms and the agents go to their hiding places. The detective then explains the game to the students and divides them into groups. She then hands out copies of the Clue Sheet Checklist (see sample), golf pencils, and $500 worth of play money to each student. Once these items are distributed, the game begins.

Students play in groups of two to four. They must search the church to find the hidden agents in order to get the clues that will lead them to the evidence with which they can solve the murder and win the game. The primary activity of a group should be to locate the secret agents and keep guessing (and answering challenge questions) until a solution to one of the categories (suspect, victim, weapon, room, motive) is discovered. In this way,

the group may discover the answers to all five parts of the crime, which will enable them to obtain the four passwords from the motive agent and use them to locate the evidence.

If a group so chooses, they may attempt to bribe the suspects into disclosing information (as discussed later on). However, the group must always check the information obtained from a suspect with the agent who is knowledgeable about that category, or else the group will not get all four passwords.

After finding the answers to all five categories and obtaining the passwords, the students must figure out the meaning of the passwords in order to find the evidence. The detective may assist in this. Once a group presents the correct evidence to the detective, they win the game.

The suspects are located in the rooms that correspond to their names on the Clue Sheet Checklist and they should have in their possession the corresponding weapons. So, using the example from the sample Clue Sheet Checklist, Jackknife John will be in the parlor holding the duct tape. However, the trio of suspect/victim, weapon, and motive are not necessarily related, and students should be made aware of this fact.

The function of the suspects is to play their roles as shady characters (in other words, possible suspects) throughout the game. This mainly means providing inside information...for a price. Students can use the money they received at the start of the game, if they so choose, to bribe suspects into sharing what they know. Since the actors will already know the solution to the mystery, the suspects can provide whatever information they deem to be worth the price they're paid. For example, for $100

SAMPLE

CLUE SHEET CHECKLIST

SUSPECTS	VICTIMS	WEAPONS	ROOMS	MOTIVES
Dastardly Deb	Dastardly Deb	Guitar	Club Room	Bad Sermon
Jackknife John	Jackknife John	Duct Tape	Parlor	Musikfest Overload
Ruthless Ruthie	Ruthless Ruthie	Nail Polish	Youth Lounge	Left Toilet Seat Up
Lisping Laura	Lisping Laura	Cow Head	Room 184	Wasted Water
Erroneous Eileen	Erroneous Eileen	Frisbee	Kitchen	Slept through Class

| _____ | _____ | _____ | _____ | _____ |
| (password) | (password) | (password) | (password) | (password) |

they may want to discount one of the five possibilities, for $250 they could give hints for an answer, and for $500 they might provide the answer to one of the five categories. As shady characters, the suspects aren't always to be trusted and can also choose to mislead players with their answers. And any answers they give will have to be checked out with the secret agents.

Students will receive an additional $100 each time they discover the answer for one of the five items (suspect, victim, weapon, room, motive). So to narrow down the list, they must find the five secret agents who are situated in fixed hiding places that are known only by the detective. The hiding places should range in degree of difficulty to be discovered by the students. (Place the agent in charge of motive in the most obscure hiding place.)

The function of the agents is to provide the students with information based on their areas of expertise. Agents may not be bribed and aren't allowed to provide answers to questions that aren't within their areas of expertise. If players ask them questions about a category other than the ones they've been assigned, they should respond, "I don't know." Then the students are allowed to ask other questions until they figure out which categories this agent is knowledgeable about.

In order to obtain the help of the secret agents, students must first find their hiding spots, and then ask specific questions based on the agents' areas of expertise. For example, students might ask, "Was Jackknife John the murderer?" If students guess incorrectly, the agent asks them to answer one of the challenge questions on their sheet (see sample). These scavenger-hunt questions encourage students to move around, while preventing them from continuously questioning the same agent. Each agent needs

---

SAMPLE AGENTS' CHALLENGE QUESTIONS

How many rows of pews are in the sanctuary?	26
How many candles are on one chandelier in the sanctuary?	24
Which row of pews has a red cross?	14
How many fan blades are in Fellowship Hall?	30
How many couches are in room 170?	3
Where do the paisley arrows lead?	Room 178
How many hymnals are in the chapel?	80 (81)
How many squares long is the foul line in the gym?	24
To whom is the statue outside the Kirk Center dedicated?	Keith Brown
What is the color of the dot used on Old Testament books in the Resource Center?	Orange
What is the color of the carpet in room 412?	Green
What are the hours that dial-a-ride is available?	8 am–noon
How many folding chairs are on the balcony?	14
What is the number on the dumpster?	8597
How many slides are on the playground?	4
How many parking spaces wide is the parking lot?	59
What is the license plate of the blue and white van?	OB-29224

---

only four challenge questions to use during the game, as there are only five possible answers that players might guess for each category. When the players return with the information the agent requested, then they have permission to ask another question or make another guess about that category's solution.

If the students guess correctly, the agent gives them $100 and places his "mark" on one of the small lines on the checklist. The agent with information about the suspects places her mark on the line under suspects, the one dealing with the victims places his mark on the line under victims, and so on. However, the agent assigned to the motive doesn't place a mark on the checklist. Instead, she provides passwords that will help the students locate the evidence to win the game. An example of a password you could use is "Cross Pew Friendship Booklet." Although fairly obscure, when read by a skilled detective, this phrase indicates that the evidence is located in the friendship booklet in the pew with the small, red cross painted on it. Passwords are provided only after a group correctly guesses the motive and has obtained the other four agents' marks.

When a group finds the picture that proves the murder, they must take it to the detective, who will then make an arrest and reward the winning group.

The detective is free to wander around the church during the course of the game in order to assist the students and actors with any problems they may encounter. He should carry with him a megaphone and a large amount of extra play money. Most importantly, his role is to clarify any questions that may arise and to tell students the next step they should take if they're confused. Groups who can't seem to find the agents can ask the detective to show them the location of one of them. And the detective can choose to give financial assistance to other groups who are significantly behind the rest. They'll need to give the detective a "good story" as to why they need more money, though.

The detective should also make the rounds to visit the suspects and heckle them in the presence of students. If body outlines have not been made prior to starting the game, the detective can also go around taping outlines on the floors of the possible murder locations. Occasionally, the detective should check up on the agents to see if things are going well.

Deputies and Photographers perform similar roles as the detective, but they don't have any money to distribute. If there are enough leaders, each group of students can have a deputy (a leader who doesn't know the solutions) to lead them in their search for the murderer.

If you have an abundance of leaders who don't want to lead groups of students as deputies, you can have two or three protected witnesses to the murder. These folks are living under the witness protection program, so they should dress in disguise and hide themselves very well in the church. If students happen to find a witness, they may attempt to get that person to disclose information. However, the students must remember that the witnesses are hiding for their lives and may be reluctant to share what they know. The best way to gain their favor is to promise that their locations will remain secret. Witnesses must always tell the truth.

The game concludes with the detective making a very public arrest of the murderer. The winning team is given medals of valor for solving the crime. Take some pictures of the students with their favorite suspects or secret agents as souvenirs of the game. *Laura Dubinski and Joshua Gieske*

Mako Aajo Cultural Exchange

If your youth group could benefit from some sensitivity training—and what group of teens couldn't?—try this exercise. It may help them to experience what it feels like to be a stranger or an outsider in a new group. Divide the group into two smaller ones, with at least eight players in each. One group will be the Mako culture, and the other will be the Aajo culture. Place your immature, noncommunicative, or easily bored students into the Mako group because the level of activity will hold their interest longer.

The two groups will play in two separate rooms. Assign a couple of adult staff members to each group. They should enthusiastically read aloud the cultural instruction sheets and then be available to explain the instructions again if kids seem confused. Take a moment now to read the instructions yourself on pages 139-140.

The cultural assistants will also be responsible for handing out Uno cards to the players (remove the action cards). Depending on the size of your group, you'll need a couple of packs of cards per culture. Each Mako gets 10 Uno cards, and each Aajo gets six. The Aajos also need index cards and pencils to use during the game. And the leader in the Mako room will need to keep score somewhere where everyone can see it—a dry erase board, overhead transparency and projector, chalkboard, flip chart, whatever.

You can intensify the effects of this game by tweaking the behavioral expectations a little bit. For the Mako culture, for example, you could add that anyone can scream out the score at regular intervals—shorter ones as the game winds down—and loudly play some wild music in the background. In the Aajo culture you could serve refreshments and play quiet, soothing music.

After the kids have been playing in their own cultures for about 20 minutes (or less time if they get restless and bored quickly), exchange two or three players between the two groups. Don't explain to the visitors how their new cultures behave—just allow them to observe the action and try to figure it out on their own. Let the "exchange students" stay in the foreign cultures long enough to get the feel of being strangers, but not so long that they get bored. Then send them back to their own cultures and choose a few new students to visit.

After all the players have visited the other cultures, end the game and bring the two groups back together for a time of debriefing. Ask the players about their experiences during the game and what they thought about the other groups. Share from Leviticus 19:33-34 about how God wants us to treat outsiders or "aliens" living among us. You could also use Matthew 25:35-40 to discuss the proper treatment of strangers and those in need.

Don't underestimate the powerful impact this game can have on teenagers. *Michl Kohl*

BIFFERS

The object of the game is for the students to find and obtain the signatures of 10 volunteers who are hidden throughout the church or playing area. Once a volunteer is found, she can ask the student to perform some silly task to pay for finding her, like answering Bible trivia questions or doing 15 jumping jacks while singing "Jesus Loves Me." Each player needs a piece of paper, and the signature volunteers need pens.

While the kids are trying to get all 10 signatures on their papers, four "biffers" are roaming around with flour-filled socks waiting to tag players. Once a player is hit or "biffed," he must stop where he is and yell for a medic. When one of the three medics comes to his aid, the medic uses a colored marker or pen to draw a cross on the back of the player's hand so he can resume playing. The game continues until a kid gets all 10 signatures.

You could use this game as a lead-in to a talk about how life sometimes "biffs" us while we're running around trying to get things done—homework, jobs, time with family, extracurricular activities, and so on. Sometimes we're stopped in our tracks by things like sin, Satan's spiritual attacks, and bad choices. But when we call on the Lord (the medics), he'll help us get going again. And we can call on God because Jesus died on the cross for us (thus, the crosses on the backs of the players' hands). God may not always come at the moment we think he should, but he's always there and we're not forgotten. *Julie Luedthe*

THE PLAGUE

If the elders of your church will let you have the run of the building, try this chaotic, church-wide game. Purchase three different colors of small, round adhesive labels or stickers (we've used white, green, and red in our examples that follow) so you have two to five per student. Your adult leaders will be major participants in this game. Assign the role of "nurse" to two of them.

Divide the youth group into two teams, and give each player a white label to attach to her shirt. Let the students loose in the church and see how long they can avoid "The Plague"—the adult leaders. The staff should give the students a two-minute head start before going after them. When a leader finds a student, he should tag the kid by confiscating her white label and giving her a red one to signify that she's been caught by The Plague. Students are required to stand motionless wherever they were caught. Before they can rejoin the game they must call out, "Nurse!"

The two nurses should roam the building. Their job is to heal the infected players by removing the red labels and replacing them with green ones. Students who receive green labels are allowed to return to the game. However, if those green-labeled students are caught once more by The Plague, they must hand over their green labels and cry out for the nurse again.

When it's time to wrap up the game, call all the students back together and have them turn in their labels for points. To make the scoring process easier, have a sheet of paper on hand for each team. As the labels are turned in, simply attach them to the team's paper. White labels receive 100 points each, and green labels earn 50 points. However, each red label deducts 25 points from the team's total score. Add up the points and declare a winner. *Jeff Hicks*

SLAPSTICK ASSASSIN

This is an ongoing game that will take place outside your youth group meeting times. Students who wish to play should print—not sign—their names on both a sign-up sheet and a sheet of stickers or mailing labels. Have kids personally hand their stickers to an adult staff member, to avoid the confusion of

Instructions for the Mako Culture

From now on you are a Mako! Being a Mako is not as easy as it sounds. There are a lot of rules, many duties, and few rights. As a Mako you want only two things: work and success. All Makos are incredible workaholics. Your motto in life: I want it all!

Your work is swapping cards. By doing so in a clever way, you can accumulate points, and every Mako wants to get as many points as possible.

You'll each receive 10 cards, and you have to collect rows of numbers of the same color of card. Keep your card collection lying facedown in front of you so no one can see your cards. If you have three cards of the same color and in the right sequence, the numbers will be added together to get your total score. So if you have three green cards numbered four, five, and six, your score is 15 points. Every time you score a row of cards, turn the cards in so your score can be recorded on the scoreboard up front for all to see. Then get some new cards so you can start playing again.

You probably won't have the cards you need to score a row at first, so you need to swap cards with your fellow Makos. Hold the cards you're willing to swap in one hand. A swap can be done only if the Mako you approach wants to swap with you as well. You can't take a card from a Mako without giving that person one in return. During a swap you shouldn't touch anybody and you must wait until you've made eye contact with someone before making your request. Never point! It's embarrassing. Makos also look very foolish when they count or add up numbers on their fingers.

When you talk about swapping cards, you must use the Mako language, which only consists of the syllables you need for swapping—nothing more. First say the color of the cards you need, but only the first two letters of the color name because you haven't got much time! For example, *gr* for green, *bl* for blue, and *re* for red.

As for the number of the card you need, you use only syllables to express this as well. Take the first letters of your first and last name, and put an *a* after the first and an *o* after the second. So if your name is Michael Kohl, your syllables are *ma ko*. And if your name is Susie Smith, your syllables are *sa so*. Just say the two syllables when you make your request, and do it as many times as necessary to equal the number on the card you seek.

Now let's put it all together. Say you want a yellow three card. You would say, "Ye ma ko ma." *Ye* is for *yellow*, and the three syllables *ma ko ma* because you want a number-three card. If you wanted a red five card, you'd say, "Re ma ko ma ko ma." A green two card? "Gr ma ko." How about the blue four card—"Bl ma ko ma ko." Are you with me now?

If you use a different language, like English, or touch a Mako at any point during the game, you will get a two-minute time ban, during which you can't swap any cards. That's a big downer for a Mako! It's also forbidden for you to speak anything other than the Mako language while visiting with another group. You're not allowed to explain any of the Mako cultural rules to them. If you do, you'll receive a five-minute time ban with swapping restrictions.

Instructions for the Aajo Culture

I warmly welcome you as a highly honored and valuable member of the culture of Aajos. How are you today? All members of the Aajo culture are very glad you're with them today. Everybody is interested in who you really are and how you're doing.

To be an Aajo is easy. For Aajos the most important things are getting to know each other and building relationships. That's how Aajos are. Your desire is to get to know the members of the Aajo culture better.

But there are a few rules. Each Aajo gets six cards for swapping. There are always two Aajos swapping cards. To do this, hold up your cards and let your fellow Aajo pick one and place it faceup in front of her. Now it's your turn to pick one of her cards and place it in front of you, also faceup. The one who chose the higher card is allowed to give his card to the other Aajo.

When you run out of cards, go get some more. It doesn't matter because the most important part of the action comes before the swapping: You're allowed to talk to each other about anything at all. Think of a few things you've always wanted to ask each other. Here's your chance! No Aajo would ever lie.

If you enjoy the talk with your fellow Aajo and feel you really got into a good conversation, sign that person's conversation card with your full name. On the other hand, if you have the feeling that your fellow Aajo wasn't really into the conversation and wasn't very interested in you, write a number on the card to represent how well you thought the conversation went on a scale from one to 10. Your conversation partner will have a chance to sign or number your conversation card as well.

A conversation card full of numbers is very embarrassing to an Aajo because it tells your fellow Aajos that you're not really good at making conversation. So after you've talked to every Aajo in the group, take a short break and then try talking again with those Aajos who gave you numbers. This time, try to receive full signatures from them by being an attentive listener and expressing great interest in what they're saying to you. Give it your best effort.

If you do anything other than what you're allowed to do as an Aajo—especially during your visits to the Mako culture—you will get a two-minute time ban. During this time no one will be allowed to talk to you and you can't talk to anyone else. This is a big downer for an Aajo. And if you explain the rules of your Aajo culture to any Mako, you'll get a five-minute time ban.

students who don't want to play being signed up by fellow students.

After the sign-ups are over, on a sheet of paper list all the names of the players in random order. The target for each assassin will be the person whose name follows his on the sheet you just created. The target for the last person on the list is the person at the top of the list. Keep this list strictly confidential so no one has an unfair advantage.

Cut apart the labels and distribute them to the proper assassins. Tell them they must carry their labels with them at all times. The objective for each assassin is to eliminate the person whose name is on her sticker. This is done by placing the sticker on her target's back. When a player has successfully eliminated her target, the person who was assassinated must sign the sticker under his printed name and give the assassin his target's sticker.

There are certain restrictions that must be noted regarding the assassination attempts:

- The sticker must be placed on the person's back, or it doesn't count. If a sticker ends up on a shirt-sleeve or pant leg instead, the assassin must take the sticker back.

- If an attempt is made but fails, the assassin can't try again until 24 hours later.

- There must be at least one witness present to validate that the target was eliminated. Therefore, assassins may wish to bring along their own witnesses when they go in for a kill. However, there usually isn't much of a debate when a target has been stuck properly.

You could include some rules about the assassination attempts not counting if they're done inside the church, in a house, in a classroom, or within 15 minutes before or after a scheduled church event. This way potential targets will have some moments when they know they can relax and stop looking over their shoulders!

Before the happy assassin can move on to his next target, he must call the point person (a leader who has sole possession of the sign-up sheet) and report the name of the player that he's just eliminated from the game. The point person should cross off students' names as they're terminated. This will help the adult staff keep track of who's still playing.

The game continues until only one assassin remains. For a group of 60 kids, it could take four to

five weeks to complete, depending on how the kids get into it. When played with more than a hundred people, it may take a few months to finish. *Kirk Killinger*

CAPTURE THE TAPE

In an area the size of a football field, the group is broken into two teams and each group is assigned a color—red versus blue, green versus yellow, whatever. Each player is given a six-inch piece of colored electrical tape—the same color as the team, of course. The tape must be worn on the front of players' shirts. Adult players are given 12-inch pieces to wear, which are worth extra points.

The two teams start on opposite ends of the playing field. The objective is for players to get the pieces of tape off their opponents while protecting their own pieces. When a player loses his tape, he's out. Boys may not take tape off girls' shirts, and adult leaders can't capture anyone's tape.

When the game is over—usually when you've run out of time—each team counts the pieces of tape in their possession. Six-inch pieces are worth one point, 12-inch pieces are worth five or 10 points. The team with the most points wins.

SQUIRT GUN WARS

Here's a wetter version of Capture the Flag you can try. Each player gets paper targets safety-pinned to her front and back—so you need at least two targets per player. Make the targets out of half-sheets of paper and use watercolor markers to color a large three- to four-inch square in the center of each paper. Players also need squirt guns—Super Soakers work best, but any kind will do—and arm bands or another way to designate who's on which team. (See **Team ID** on page 19 for an easy team-identification idea.)

Each group hides a flag somewhere on their side of the playing area. When the signal is given, each team begins to search for their opponent's flag. When members of opposing teams meet up with each other, they should start shooting their squirt guns until someone's target gets wet and the color starts to run. Just one wet and runny target—front or back—is enough to send a player to the refill area.

The refill area is a neutral zone with some kind

of water supply—a kiddie pool full of water, a lake or pond, or even buckets full of water—anything the kids can use to refill their squirt guns. Also keep a supply of dry targets for the players to exchange for their wet ones after they've been hit. Mark the boundaries of the neutral refill area with flour, orange safety cones, ropes, or whatever boundary-marking supplies you've got handy.

As soon as a player has a new target pinned on him, he's free to rejoin the game. If a player is carrying her opponent's flag back to base when she's hit, she must drop the flag and go get a new target. Once a person is hit, he may not shoot anyone else on his way to the refill area. No shooting is allowed within the boundaries of the refill area, either.

When a flag is found and safely brought to the refill area, that round is over. Sound the signal for all the players to return to the refill zone, announce the winner, and then make preparations to start the next round of the game. *Sandy Lazenby*

GLOW-STICK CAPTURE THE FLAG

For a nighttime variation of Capture the Flag, rope off a wooded area, use glow sticks instead of flags, and ask the kids to wear dark clothing and bring their own ammunition—plastic baggies filled with flour, water balloons, balloons full of shaving cream, eggs, and so on.

Divide the kids into two teams, and split the ammunition between them. Before the game begins, send each team to their side of the playing area to hide their glow stick where it's still somewhat visible.

When you give the signal, the teams begin the hunt. The goal is to sneak around, find the opponent's glow stick, and bring it back to your team's home base situated somewhere outside the boundaries of the playing field. And if you should come across your opponent in the dark, you try to tag that person with your ammunition. When a player is hit with a flour bag, an egg, or another messy weapon—the player is out for that round and must leave the playing area. If that player had the glow stick in her possession when she was tagged, she has to drop it and go. One of her teammates could try to pick it up and head for home base. Or whoever tagged her could retrieve the glow stick and hide it somewhere new.

Once an opponent's glow stick has been safely delivered to a team's headquarters, signal the end of that round. All the players should return to their headquarters and prepare for another round.

ONE-ARMED MAN

With an even number of girls and guys, a large outdoor area in which to run around, and the cover of darkness—this game works great with any size group.

The guys' team is called The Fugitives. Give each male player a flag-football harness with one flag or strips of fabric he can loosely tuck into his pockets. The girls' team is called The Law. Give each female player a flashlight and provide the team with a couple of walkie-talkies, if possible. Finally, choose a staff person to be "the one-armed man."

Give the staff person a few minutes' head start to find his hiding place somewhere within the boundaries of the playing area. It's best if he hides well enough to make the game fun, but not so well that it's impossible to find him. Now have The Law spread out on the playing field. Once the girls find the one-armed man, only three girls may guard him.

Now release The Fugitives from their headquarters. Their job is to search for The One-Armed Man. Once the guys find the staff person, they let him tear off their flags (this gives their team points) and head back to headquarters to get new flags. Meanwhile, members of The Law will also try to rip off the guys' flags, using whatever means necessary. Any guy who isn't in headquarters is fair game, but no girl can be within 50 feet of The Fugitives' headquarters. The guys' only defense against the girls is their speed! Anytime a guy loses his flag—to the one-armed man or to The Law—he must return to headquarters for a new one.

The game should last 20 to 30 minutes. At the end, give the signal for everyone to return to headquarters. The Law and the one-armed man should give their retrieved flags to a staff person to count. Both teams receive 100,000 points for every flag they turn in. The team with the most points at the end wins. *Jayson Turner*

ENHANCE ANY NIGHT GAME

To spice up some of your favorite after-dark games, buy some army face paint or low-end theatrical face paint (the kind that clowns and mimes use). The make-up is reasonably inexpensive, and your students—especially junior highers—will love putting it on themselves and each other. Make sure the kids wear old clothes, though. The paint is oil-based and gets really messy if too much is applied. Along with a new variation of an old game, you'll get some great photos to display. *Jayson Turner*

OWL

Divide the group into teams of four or five. Each team picks a call and an answer for their group. For example, "This little light of mine…" could be the call, and the answer would be "I'm gonna let it shine!" Or a team could use "Jesus loves me…" and "This I know!" or "Father Abraham…" and "Had many sons!" Once the call and answer have been established, each team chooses one member to be the "owl." Then choose five or six adult staff people to be the snipers, and arm them with Nerf dart guns or other similarly harmless weapons and ammunition.

Owls are given five minutes to hide in the woods or somewhere in the church if playing indoors. They don't have to stay in one spot during the game. During this time, release the snipers and let them scatter around the playing area.

Now the teams are free to go find their owls. They do this by yelling out their calls and then listening for their owls to answer. When they hear the owls respond, they try to track them down by following the sounds of their voices.

Meanwhile, the snipers are out and about, ready to shoot any team members they choose. If a player is hit by a sniper, she has to go back to her team's main base until the next round. Snipers will eventually learn the teams' calls and answers and use this information to confuse the teams as to where their owls are hiding. Snipers aren't allowed to shoot the owls, though. The first team to find their owl and safely escort him back to the main base wins. Or let the owl who hides the longest without being found win. *EE*

SNIPE HUNTING

Have you heard about snipe hunting? Snipes are those pretend bird-like animals that live in the woods and run along the ground at night. To successfully play this game, you have to be willing to use your imagination and then get the kids worked up to use theirs as well. When they actually believe you're catching snipes, they'll buy it and love it!

It's important to have the right atmosphere for this game. First, it must be dark outside and late at night. The moon should be semi-bright so you can at least see where you're walking. No flashlights are allowed, and everyone should dress in dark-colored clothing. You must also be in the woods or some other shadowy place—not out in wide-open spaces. Finally, there should be some large rocks on the ground where you're playing.

Before you head to the snipe-hunting grounds, you need the proper snipe-hunting gear: a large cloth sack with a drawstring around the top. You can even make it look more official by placing the words "Snipe Sack" on the outside.

Get the kids pumped up about this adventure. Tell them you realize that some people may not believe that snipes exist—but they're real! Give them time and they'll get excited.

Have the kids apply the all-important snipe neutralizer—bug spray. It's no fun to be out in the woods and get eaten alive by bugs. Tell the kids that the spray will disguise their human scent, which is important because snipes can sniff that out in an instant!

Now teach the snipe call. This is the call you must shout loudly in order to attract the snipes into your sack. It's the snipe mating call and will make the snipe run right into the bag. Roll your tongue when you make this sound, "Rrrrrrr-eye! Eye! Eye!" And the louder the better! Make sure you have students practice this. In fact, really gear them up for this. The louder you shout, the sooner you'll catch a snipe.

Now head outside. When you get to the hunting spot, explain that it's important for only a few kids to be with you at a time. Snipes come out only at night and can smell people, so the fewer kids there are on the hunt, the greater your chances for success. In reality, you don't want to have the whole group with you at once because one kid will be sure to see what you're really doing and ruin the whole thing. Plus, making groups of kids wait their turn is a good way to build the anticipation. So leave some kids sitting in a dark spot at a distance from you. They may be scared, but that's one of the risks and challenges of snipe hunting.

Explain the snipe-hunting stance. You're the chief hunter, so you'll hold the sack at all times. Four kids (or however many you choose) should stand around you—two on each side—as you crouch low to the ground with the mouth of the sack opened away from you. Tell them that while they're hunting with you, they must keep their eyes closed and shout the snipe call. Snipes have incredible vision and will not only smell them, but see the reflection of moonlight in their eyes. So the kids must keep their eyes shut at all times, unless you say otherwise. (See **For a Better Snipe Hunt** for more important pointers about snipe hunting.)

Now the hunting begins. Have one of your hands on the drawstring of the sack and be ready to pull hard to close it. Here's the kicker—in your other hand, hold a medium-size or larger rock. This is actually the snipe. So on the count of three, with everyone's eyes shut tight, you'll shout the snipe call repeatedly and loudly! Repeat it at least four times or more. Then when the time is right, toss the rock into the sack and quickly close it as you start to scream. You've caught a snipe!

Now stand up and start to throw or jerk the sack around while still holding onto it, as if there's a fierce wild animal inside. Get into it! Say things like "I can't believe I caught a snipe!" or "Can you see it moving? It's huge!" or "This is the first snipe I've ever actually caught!" or "I wish my dad could see this! He'd be soooo jealous!" The more jazzed you are about this, the more excited the kids will get.

When everyone is convinced there's a snipe in the bag, say, "Okay, everyone, get back! I'm gonna let this baby go!" If the kids protest and want to see the snipe, say, "Oh no! The snipe will jump out and bite. It's very dangerous. So I'm going to turn away from you and let the snipe out onto the ground."

FOR A BETTER SNIPE HUNT

How to handle the occasional questions about snipe hunting:

- Snipes are very strong and they bite very hard! Therefore, only you can hold the sack. No kids are allowed to, as snipe hunting requires strength. Play off of this. It works. Also, you've been trained how to handle the sack and how to defend yourself against the snipe attacks. Snipe hunting is an art—only a few know how to do it correctly, and you're one of those few, of course.

- Snipes come out only at night. They hide deep in the ground during the day. So you can't see them at all during daylight hours.

- Snipes have a keen sense of vision and smell. They can smell humans and will see the moon reflected in the kids' eyes. And no flashlights are allowed!

- You've been snipe hunting for years and you've caught only a few snipes (depending on your age). In fact, you may not have caught any at all before this night, so you need the kids' help to catch one now!

- No one hunts snipe alone. Snipes run toward a loud mating call; therefore, more than one person is necessary to make a noise loud enough to attract them.

- The game takes time and patience. Hunting can take a long time. Make sure the kids are prepared to be outside for a while.

- The kids must be very quiet at all times, except when they're shouting the mating call. Kids who are loud throughout the game will ruin the hunting experience for everyone else.

- Make sure you don't play with kids who know what you're doing or who've played with you before. In other words, you can't play this game every week with the same kids unless they still have no clue!

- Never, ever, ever give your hunting tips away. Never tell kids what you're really doing. Once they become youth leaders or camp counselors, you may wish share the truth with them if they'd like to go snipe hunting with their own groups of kids or campers.

- If parents question what you're up to, just tell them it's a fun and harmless game. *Mary Fletcher*

Remind them that snipes smell humans and will see the moon's reflection in their eyes. Then walk away from the group into a dark spot and gently empty the sack. Pretend you see the snipe dash away. Then stand and say something like "Wow! That was incredible! I can't believe we caught one that easily! Are you guys ready to try again?"

Now it's the rest of the kids' turn. By this point they'll be more than ready to try it. You can catch one as easily as you want to. Sometimes you'll catch one on the first 10 snipe calls, sometimes it takes up to 30. Use your creative juices here. Remember—the louder the better! Don't forget to go back to get a new group of amateur snipe hunters so you can repeat the hunting lesson. *Mary Fletcher*

STRAW IN A HAYSTACK

Here's an outdoor, after-dark game that's a variation on the game Mission Impossible. Kids can play either on teams or "every man for himself." On one side of the playing area, set up a station where the kids will receive a peanut, a toothpick, another small object. Twist ties work well because the kids must wear them around their fingers and cannot take them off or otherwise hide them in an effort to cheat during the game.

On the signal, students enter the playing area and try to find two token-carriers hiding somewhere within the boundaries. These players can wear glow sticks around their necks to distinguish them from other players.

Once a player finds a token-carrier, she trades in her peanut to get a drinking straw, a rubber band, a sticker, a button, or a similar object before returning to the starting point. If she gets back safely and hands over her straw, she'll receive points for the new object.

For a variation, use several token-carriers. Each can wear a different-colored glow stick and hold a bag full of different objects for trades (make each object worth a different point value). One could have buttons, another rubber bands, a third drinking straws, and so on. So a player starts out with a twist tie and must make a trade with each token-carrier, then turn in his traded objects back at headquarters to win.

But there's a catch (there's always a catch!).

Adult staff members with flashlights, called "gunners," are out and about trying to catch the kids. If a player is hit with a beam of light by the gunner, he cannot run away from the gunner. Instead, he must relinquish whatever object he's holding at the time and the player gets zero points for that exchange. The players who've been caught by the gunners must return to the starting point, get new peanuts, twist ties, or other objects, and restart their quest.

Another variation is to give each gunner a roll of duct tape to carry. When a gunner catches one of the players, she not only confiscates the player's token, but she also gets to duct tape the player. And if the kid makes a run for it, all the gunner has to do is shout, and the other gunners will join in the pursuit. Very seldom does a student escape, and then he gets taped up even more because he tried to run.

Make some rules about where the gunners can put tape on the kids, like no taping above the neck or putting tape on bare skin. They can be as creative as they like in their tape jobs by mummifying players or taping one hand to a leg. And if they catch two or three players at once, they can tape them together. However, the number-one rule is that the kids are playing for fun, so let them win a few, even though it would be really easy for the adults to catch all the youths. The team or individual who finishes with the most points wins. *Jason Hofer*

ROMANS AND CHRISTIANS

Here's an effective, hands-on way to give your students a little background about the difficult lives of Roman Christians who were persecuted and sometimes killed for their faith. This game works best with older students, and it's amazing to see them get into it. If possible, play this at night in a large, outdoor area with lots of trees. Make sure the kids are prepared ahead of time with old clothes, enough clothes (if it's cold), bug spray (if it's warm), and so on. If you must play inside, it has to be really dark. The game can take up to two hours to complete.

Kids are Christians, and adult staff members are Romans. The Christians are on a mission to find the "light" (a tiki torch, campfire, or candle) that's hidden in some part of the playing area. It must be difficult for them to find. You also need to establish an area that will serve as the prison, guarded by a

145

Roman guard.

The Romans have flashlights and use them to hunt for the Christians. If they find and "beam" the Christians, the Romans yell at the kids in a very loud voice, "Christian! Where are you, Christian?" and so on, and the captured players are sent to prison. In order to get out of prison, the kids must witness to the jail guard (another adult staff member) until that guard is convinced that there's a God and lets the Christians go. To earn their freedom, the Christians cannot use simple claims like "God loves you" or sing "Jesus Loves Me." They must either recite Scripture, tell a Bible story about God's love or about Jesus, or share a personal faith story.

The goal of the game is to get as many Christians to the light (in other words, salvation or heaven) as possible. If a Christian makes it to the light, she can either stay there or go back to help other Christians find it. Christians can also take the risk of trying to convert Roman soldiers with more Bible stories, Scripture, and so on. The witnessing must be really good for that to happen, though. If a Roman soldier does convert, he may now work to help the Christians get other Christians to the light hidden behind the other Romans.

After the game, bring the kids together to wrap up and debrief the experience with them. Discuss how they felt and what it was like to witness to people who were after them. See if they'll tell you what the hardest part of being a Christian is today. There are a lot of similarities between the Roman era and the present day that you can use to illustrate and teach. Close with prayer, and thank God for the Christians who sacrificed their lives for our faith.

Mary Fletcher

POLAROID CAPTURE THE FLAG

It should be a dark and stormy night—okay, just dark. Divide your group into two teams, and put them at opposite ends of a large playing area, such as a school campus or church property. Each team member has a flashlight, and each team has one Polaroid camera. Identify the game area's physical boundaries to the players. Leaders should circulate and closely monitor the game as it plays out, so there's no illegal activity like dragging people around or holding people down till they tell where the Polaroid person is—not that the kids would even think of doing such things!

The object of the game is for one Polaroid person to get a clear picture of the other team's Polaroid person, as judged by the youth leader. Team members hunt for the other team's Polaroid person. They also try to take out members of the other team by flashing them with their flashlights. A person who's been flashed is out of the game and goes to a neutral location (preferably someplace where they can still see the game unfolding—but be guarded by a leader so they don't shout help to their team about the other team's Polaroid person). A Polaroid person can't be taken out by flashing—which identifies them as the other team's Polaroid person. Also, a Polaroid person can't lie. So if a team member catches someone from the other team and asks if they're the Polaroid person, the real Polaroid person has to say yes.

A variation on this game is to have team members defend their own holding areas. Defenders get flashlights and can "beam" and capture anyone from the other team who might wander by innocently. Each team's holding area should be monitored by a leader. If a member of Team A sneaks up to Team B's holding area and tags a Team B defender, one member of Team A is freed. These two Team A members have 20 seconds to get away from the holding area and back in play before they can be chased by Team B defenders (and the defenders obviously can't go far). The object of the game is the same—for one Polaroid person to get a clear picture of the other.

Another adaptation for larger groups or smaller budgets (as flashlights for everyone can get expensive) is to substitute flour-filled pantyhose legs. These leave an easily visible (and reasonably painless) mark on people's clothes. Those who get whacked go to the holding area.

RESOURCES FROM YOUTH SPECIALTIES

Youth Ministry Programming

Camps, Retreats, Missions, & Service Ideas (Ideas Library)

Compassionate Kids: Practical Ways to Involve Your Students in Mission and Service

Creative Bible Lessons from the Old Testament

Creative Bible Lessons in 1 & 2 Corinthians

Creative Bible Lessons in John: Encounters with Jesus

Creative Bible Lessons in Romans: Faith on Fire!

Creative Bible Lessons on the Life of Christ

Creative Bible Lessons in Psalms

Creative Junior High Programs from A to Z, Vol. 1 (A-M)

Creative Junior High Programs from A to Z, Vol. 2 (N-Z)

Creative Meetings, Bible Lessons, & Worship Ideas (Ideas Library)

Crowd Breakers & Mixers (Ideas Library)
Downloading the Bible Leader's Guide

Drama, Skits, & Sketches (Ideas Library)

Drama, Skits, & Sketches 2 (Ideas Library)

Dramatic Pauses

Everyday Object Lessons

Games (Ideas Library)

Games 2 (Ideas Library)

Good Sex: A Whole-Person Approach to Teenage Sexuality & God

Great Fundraising Ideas for Youth Groups

More Great Fundraising Ideas for Youth Groups

Great Retreats for Youth Groups

Holiday Ideas (Ideas Library)

Hot Illustrations for Youth Talks

More Hot Illustrations for Youth Talks

Still More Hot Illustrations for Youth Talks

Ideas Library on CD-ROM

Incredible Questionnaires for Youth Ministry

Junior High Game Nights

More Junior High Game Nights

Kickstarters: 101 Ingenious Intros to Just about Any Bible Lesson

Live the Life! Student Evangelism Training Kit

Memory Makers

The Next Level Leader's Guide

Play It! Over 150 Great Games for Youth Groups

Roaring Lambs

So What Am I Gonna Do with My Life? Leader's Guide

Special Events (Ideas Library)

Spontaneous Melodramas

Spontaneous Melodramas 2

Student Leadership Training Manual

Student Underground: An Event Curriculum on the Persecuted Church

Super Sketches for Youth Ministry

Talking the Walk

Videos That Teach

What Would Jesus Do? Youth Leader's Kit

Wild Truth Bible Lessons

Wild Truth Bible Lessons 2

Wild Truth Bible Lessons—Pictures of God

Wild Truth Bible Lessons—Pictures of God 2

Worship Services for Youth Groups

Professional Resources

Administration, Publicity, & Fundraising (Ideas Library)

Dynamic Communicators Workshop for Youth Workers

Equipped to Serve: Volunteer Youth Worker Training Course

Help! I'm a Junior High Youth Worker!

Help! I'm a Small-Group Leader!

Help! I'm a Sunday School Teacher!

Help! I'm a Volunteer Youth Worker!

How to Expand Your Youth Ministry

How to Speak to Youth...and Keep Them Awake at the Same Time

Junior High Ministry (Updated & Expanded)

The Ministry of Nurture: A Youth Worker's Guide to Discipling Teenagers

Purpose-Driven Youth Ministry

Purpose-Driven Youth Ministry Training Kit

So That's Why I Keep Doing This! 52 Devotional Stories for Youth Workers

Teaching the Bible Creatively

A Youth Ministry Crash Course

Youth Ministry Management Tools
The Youth Worker's Handbook to Family Ministry

Academic Resources

Four Views of Youth Ministry & the Church
Starting Right: Thinking Theologically about Youth
Ministry

Discussion Starters

Discussion & Lesson Starters (Ideas Library)
Discussion & Lesson Starters 2 (Ideas Library)
EdgeTV
Get 'Em Talking
Keep 'Em Talking!
Good Sex: A Whole-Person Approach to Teenage
Sexuality & God
High School TalkSheets—Updated!
More High School TalkSheets—Updated!
High School TalkSheets from Psalms and Proverbs—
Updated!
Real Kids: Short Cuts
Real Kids: The Real Deal—on Friendship, Loneliness,
Racism, & Suicide
Real Kids: The Real Deal—on Sexual Choices, Family
Matters, & Loss
Real Kids: The Real Deal—on Stressing Out,
Addictive Behavior, Great Comebacks, &
Violence
Real Kids: Word on the Street
Unfinished Sentences: 450 Tantalizing Statement-
Starters to Get Teenagers Talking & Thinking
What If...? 450 Thought-Provoking Questions to Get
Teenagers Talking, Laughing, and Thinking
Would You Rather...? 465 Provocative Questions to
Get Teenagers Talking
Have You Ever...? 450 Intriguing Questions
Guaranteed to Get Teenagers Talking

Art Source Clip Art

Stark Raving Clip Art (print)
Youth Group Activities (print)
Clip Art Library Version 2.0 (CD-ROM)

Digital Resources

Clip Art Library Version 2.0 (CD-ROM)
Ideas Library on CD-ROM
Youth Ministry Management Tools (CD-ROM)

Videos & Video Curricula

Dynamic Communicators Workshop for Youth
Workers
EdgeTV
Equipped to Serve: Volunteer Youth Worker Training
Course
Good Sex: A Whole-Person Approach to Teenage
Sexuality & God
The Heart of Youth Ministry: A Morning with Mike
Yaconelli
Live the Life! Student Evangelism Training Kit
Purpose-Driven Youth Ministry Training Kit
Real Kids: Short Cuts
Real Kids: The Real Deal—on Friendship, Loneliness,
Racism, & Suicide
Real Kids: The Real Deal—on Sexual Choices, Family
Matters, & Loss
Real Kids: The Real Deal—on Stressing Out,
Addictive Behavior, Great Comebacks, &
Violence
Real Kids: Word on the Street
Student Underground: An Event Curriculum on the
Persecuted Church
Understanding Your Teenager Video Curriculum

Student Resources

Downloading the Bible: A Rough Guide to the New
Testament
Downloading the Bible: A Rough Guide to the Old
Testament
Grow For It Journal
Grow For It Journal through the Scriptures
So What Am I Gonna Do with My Life? Journaling
Workbook for Students
Spiritual Challenge Journal: The Next Level
Teen Devotional Bible
What (Almost) Nobody Will Tell You about Sex
What Would Jesus Do? Spiritual Challenge Journal
Wild Truth Journal for Junior Highers
Wild Truth Journal—Pictures of God